Knitted tea cosies

Knitted tea cosies

Jenny Occleshaw

NEW HOLLAND

contents

I was very excited when I had the opportunity to produce another tea cosy book. They are one of my favorite things to knit and when you drink tea like I do you can never be without a good tea cosy. I think a tea cosy is like a little work of art. It is an opportunity for your imagination to run wild whilst at the same time coming up with a practical object which serves a useful purpose in the world.

   The tea cosies in this book are not particularly difficult to knit and hopefully will offer something for all knitters. I would encourage everyone to experiment with their own color schemes and think about adding their own embellishments once they have got the hang of the basic tea cosy shape. This is the fun of making small projects. All items of hand knitting make great gifts but I think a knitted tea cosy is one which the receiver will treasure for a very long time so if you are ever wondering what to give someone, knit them a tea cosy. They are sure to be pleased.

I hope you enjoy knitting these tea cosies as much as I enjoyed designing and making them.

Jenny Occleshaw

This section describes the techniques required to teach you how to knit. You'll need time and patience to learn and perfect the different techniques, but with practice and determination you'll soon master the basics. It is inevitable that you will make mistakes, but that is all part of the learning process. You'll find in no time at all that you'll be knitting projects for your family, home and yourself!

How to Cast On

To begin knitting, you will need to create a foundation row of stitches on your needle by "casting on."

1. Make a slipknot by looping yarn into a pretzel shape, leaving a tail end at least three times the width of what you are knitting (if your scarf is 8 inches wide, you'll need a 24-inch-long tail). Slip knitting needle through pretzel shape, and pull yarn ends to tighten.
2. Drape tail of yarn over left thumb and working yarn (ball end) over left index finger. Use your other fingers to catch yarn lengths in left palm. Insert needle upward through the loop on your thumb.
3. With the needle, catch the working yarn that's on your index finger, and pull it through the loop on your thumb. Remove thumb from loop. Keeping yarn ends secured in palm, reposition thumb, and tighten new stitch on right-hand needle. Repeat these steps until you've cast on the required number of stitches.

The Knit Stitch

Now you have mastered casting on, you can begin to form the first of two fundamental movements in knitting, the knit stitch and the purl stitch. Knit stitch forms a flat, vertical loop on the fabric face.
1. Hold the needle with cast-on stitches in your left hand. Wrap the working yarn around your left index finger, and hold it back on the left-hand needle.

1. Insert point of right-hand needle from front to back into the first cast-on stitch on the left-hand needle, opening up a stitch.
2. Catch working yarn with right-hand needle.
3. Pull yarn through opened stitch.
4. Slip cast-on stitch off left-hand needle while holding middle finger against second cast-on stitch to ensure it does not also slip off. The stitch on the right-hand needle is the newly formed knit stitch. Continue knitting across the cast-on row. When you have emptied the last stitch from the left-hand needle (completing a row), exchange needles, returning the needle with stitching to your left hand.

The Purl Stitch

The purl stitch is the other fundamental stitch used in knitting. When you use this stitch along with the knit stitch it will form stocking stitch. This will produce fabric which is flat and smooth on one side and has slightly raised lines on the other. Once you have learned and mastered these two techniques, the stitches will form the basis for a huge range of patterns.

The purl stitch differs from the knit stitch in two fundamental ways: The working yarn is held in the front of the project instead of the back, and the needle is inserted from the back to the front instead of from front to back.

1. Hold the needle with cast-on stitches in your left hand. Wrap the working yarn (ball end) around your left index finger, and hold it in front of the work.
2. Insert point of right-hand needle, from back to front, into the first cast-on stitch on the left-hand needle, opening up a stitch.
3. Lay working yarn over needle from front to back by moving left index finger downward.
4. Push working yarn from front to back through cast-on stitch. Slip cast-on stitch off left-hand needle while holding middle finger against second cast-on stitch to ensure it does not also slip off. The stitch on right-hand needle is the newly formed purl stitch. As a purl stitch faces you, it looks like a grain of rice; its reverse side looks like a V.

How to Cast Off

These necessary steps keep stitches from unravelling once they are removed from the needle.

1. Knit two stitches. Insert left-hand needle into first stitch; lift stitch up over second stitch and off the needle. Continue knitting stitches in this manner until all stitches have been cast off. Cut working yarn, leaving a 15 cm (6-inch) long tail. Pull tail through last stitch to secure.
2. Use a yarn needle to weave tail ends of yarn through backs of several stitches, picking up only surface loops.

Knitting On a Set of 4 Needles (Knitting in the Round)

Many beginner knitters are intimidated by the process of knitting in the round because of the double-sided needles used to carry out this skill. However, as long as you know how to knit with two needles, it's really not that difficult – and then you will be able to create sweaters, hats, socks, and more, all with even seams.

You will need four double-pointed needles.

1. Cast your stitches onto 1 needle only. Divide the stitches evenly among 3 needles by slipping them onto 2 more needles.
2. Once all 3 needles have the same number of stitches, lay the needles flat on a table, loosely lined up end to end. (Your right-most needle should have the working yarn.) Make sure stitches aren't twisted; they should all face the same direction.

3. Join the needles to form a triangle as follows: Take the left needle in your left hand and the right needle in your right hand. Bring the needles together to form a triangle with the middle needle. Pick up your fourth needle. With the triangle still in place (and the working yarn on the right needle), knit the stitches onto the left needle, pulling working yarn tightly to join (see the image). You are now knitting in the round.

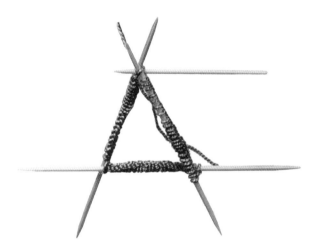

Working From a Chart

Colored patterns and designs are often charted on graph paper and make it much easier for the knitter to follow. Each square on the chart represents a stitch and each horizontal line of squares represents rows of stitches. Charts can be either colored or just black and white and they will always have a key at the side with different symbols depicting the different shades. You will read charts from bottom to top and normally from right to left. They are usually in stocking stitch and odd-numbered rows will be knit and even numbered rows will be purl, the first stitch of a chart being the bottom one on the right. Placing a straight edge of some kind, like a ruler or piece of card under each row will help you keep your place in the chart when working the design.

Tension

Tension is the resistance on the yarn as it passes through the fingers that are controlling it. Consistent, correct and exact tension is what every novice knitter is striving to achieve. Tension is THE most important thing with any garment you are going to make. This will determine the finished size of your garment, whether it fits you or is far too small or too big.

Your tension and the tension specified in the pattern must be the same so that your project will be the correct size. Before starting your project, take the time to make a tension swatch.

To check tension, using the same yarn, needles and pattern stitch specified in the instructions, make a swatch that is approximately 15 cm (6 in) square. Work in pattern for about 15 cm (6 in), and then bind off.

Let the swatch relax for a bit, and then flatten it without stretching to measure. Using pins, mark off a section of stitches in the center of the swatch that measures 10 cm (4 in) square. Count the number of stitches and rows in this 10 cm (4 in) section. If they match the tension, you can start right in on your pattern

Finishing and Making Up

Grafting

This technique is frequently used to close the toe of socks or the tips of mittens. This is an excellent way of invisibly joining two pieces of knitting. The edges are not cast off and the knitting can be joined either while it is still on the needles or after it has been taken off.

Grafting with Knitting on the Needles

- Thread a wool or tapestry needle with a length of knitting yarn. Place the two pieces to be joined with right sides facing and hold the knitting needles in the left hand.
- *Pass the wool needle knit-wise through the first stitch on the front needle and slip the stitch off the knitting needle. Pass the wool needle purl-wise through the second stitch on the same needle, leaving the stitch on the needle. Pass purl-wise through the first stitch on the back knitting needle and slip the stitch off, then pass knit-wise through the second stitch on the same needle, leaving the stitch on the needle. Repeat from*.

When following a knitting pattern you will find that the instructions contain a special vocabulary, much of it is abbreviated. It can be a little confusing when you first begin to read patterns but you will soon get to learn the different meanings. I have listed below the most common terms and their meanings. When using the patterns in this book you will refer to them. On some patterns there are special abbreviations needed but these are listed on the instructions for that particular design.

Abbreviations

K = knit

P = purl

St st = stocking stitch (USA Stockinet Stitch)

Cast Off. (USA Bind Off)

K2tog = knit 2 stitches together, thus decreasing a stitch

P2tog = purl 2 stitches together, thus decreasing a stitch

Tbl = through back of loop

Alt = alternate

Beg = beginning

Inc = increase

Dec = decrease

Rep = repeat

Sts = stitches

Sl = slip

Ssk = slip 2 sts on to the right hand needle and knit together

Patt = pattern

Psso = pass slipped stitch over

Yfwd = yarn forward, bringing yarn to front of work between the two needles, this creates a stitch

Yrn = yarn round needle.

Yo = yarn over needle.

M1 = make 1, pick up the loop which lies between the two needles and knit into the back of it, place on right hand needle

RS = right side of work

WS = wrong side of work

Anemone

This simple style ribbed tea cosy is highlighted by a beautiful anemone flower. The yarn is a thick Patons Inca. Equivalent to a Chunky or a 14 ply. The great thing about this tea cosy is you don't have to be absolutely spot on with the yarn. A little thicker or thinner and your tea cosy will just come out a bit bigger or smaller, just be careful to also alter your needle size so that your tension remains nice and even.

- 1 x 3½ oz (100 g) ball of Patons Inca (Chunky, 14 ply) Teale
- Small amount of Green 8 ply for flower and leaf (less than 1 oz/25 g) – Yarn A
- Small amount of Mid blue 8 ply for flower (less than 1 oz/25 g) – Yarn B
- Small amount of Cream 8 ply for flower (less than 1 oz/25 g) – Yarn C
- 1 pair of 4.5mm (US 7, UK 7) knitting needles
- 1 pair of 3mm (UK 11) knitting needles
- 2, 3.75mm (US 5, UK 9) double pointed knitting needles for leaf
- Wool needle for sewing up

18 st to 4 in (10cm) worked over part on 4.5mm (US 7, UK 7) knitting needles

Using 4.5mm (US 7, UK 7) knitting needles and Patons Inca, cast on 42 sts.

1st row: *P2, K3, rep from *to last 2 sts, P2.

2nd row: *K2, P3, rep from * to last 2 sts, K2.

Rep these 2 rows until work measures 5½ in (14cm) from cast on edge ending with a second row.

Shape Top

1st row: *P2, K3tog, rep from * to last 2sts, P2. 26 sts

2nd row: *K2, P1, rep from * to last 2sts, K2.

3rd row: * P2tog, K1, rep from * to last 2sts, P2tog. 17 sts

4th row: *K1, P1, rep from * to last st, K1.

5th row: P1, *Sl 1, K1, psso, rep from * to end. 9 sts

6th row: P1, P2tog, 4 times. Cast off.

Using 2, 3mm (UK 11) double pointed knitting needles, and Green 8 ply yarn, cast on 3 sts.

1st row: * Knit, do not turn work, slide sts to other end of needle and pull yarn firmly behind the work, rep from * until "I Cord" measures ¾ in (2cm), proceed as follows –

1st row: K1, yfwd, K1, yfwd, K1.

2nd and alt rows: Knit

3rd row: K2, yfwd, K1, yfwd, K2.

5th row: K3, yfwd, K1, yfwd, K3.

7th row: K4, yfwd, K1, yfwd, K4

9th row: K5, yfwd, K1, yfwd, K5.

11th row: K6, yfwd, K1, yfwd, K6.

13th row: K7, yfwd, K1, yfwd, K7. 17 sts

15th row: Sl 1, K1, paso, K15, K2tog.

17th row: Sl 1, K1, paso, K13, K2tog.

19th row: Sl 1, K1, paso, K11, K2tog.

21st row: Sl 1, K1, paso, K9, K2tog.

23rd row: Sl 1, K1, paso, K7, K2tog.

25th row: Sl 1, K1, paso, K5, K2tog.

27th row: Sl 1, K1, paso, K3, K2tog.

29th row: Sl 1, K1, paso, K1, K2tog.

31st row: Sl 1, K2tog, paso, fasten off.

Flower

Using A 8 ply (DK) yarn and 3.00mm knitting needles cast on 5 sts.

1st row: Right side – (K1, yon, K1) in each st. 15 sts

2nd row: Purl.

3rd row: (Kfb, mb, kfb) 5 times. 25 sts

4th row: P. (1A, 3B,1A) 5 times

First Petal

1st row: Right side – K1C, using B Kfb twice, K1B, K1C, turn, 7 sts.

2nd row: P2C, using B pub twice, P1B, P2C. 9 sts

3rd row: Using C Kfb, K2C, (K1B, K1C) twice, usic C Kfb, K1C. 11 sts

Continue with C

4th row: Pfb, P8, Pfb, P1. 13 sts

5th row: K1,(Kfb, K2) 4 times. 17 sts. Beginning with a purl row work 5 rows stocking st.

11th row: Ssk twice, K9, K2tog. 13 sts

12th and 14th row: Purl

13th row: K1, Ssk, K7, K2tog, K1. 11 sts

15th row: K1, Ssk, K1, Sk2pro, K1, K2tog, K1. 7 sts

Working P2tog at each end of row and pulling yarn

through last st for a smooth finish, cast off.

2nd, 3rd, 4th, and 5th petals: With right side facing join yarn through last st and work as petal on each of 5 sts.

Making up

Join row ends of center and gather cast-on row. Work a few running sts around each bobble and pull up firmly.

To Make Up

With right sides together sew top of cosy together leaving an opening for the handle and spout. Sew lower edges together for ¾ in (2cm). Darn in all loose ends and turn cosy the right way out. Stitch the Anemone to the center top of the cosy. Sew the leaf securely under one of the petals and to the top of the cosy.

MB – Make Bobble – (K1, yo, K1, yo, K1) in next st, turn, P5, turn, K5, slip 2nd, 3rd,4th and 5th sts over first st.

S2kpo – Slip 2sts as if to K2tog, K1, pass slipped sts over.

Sew on top of tea cosy.

Cherry Ripe
Tea Cosy

This simple but effective tea cosy features beautiful bunches of cherries and a small cluster of leaves surrounding a solitary cherry on the top of the cosy. The red of the cherries is offset by the cream of the cosy. Take your time when finishing your embellishments so you get a professional finish. A little extra stitch to catch the stems of the cherries in place will ensure they remain evenly around the cosy and don't end up in a bunch around the spout.

SKILL LEVEL
Advanced knitting skills

MEASUREMENTS
To fit a 6–8 cup tea pot

MATERIALS
- 3 x 2 oz (50 g) balls of 8 ply (DK) Pure Wool Cream (I used Cleackheaton Country)
- 1 x 1 oz (25 g) ball Red 4 ply (fingering) for the Cherries
- 1 x 1 oz (25 g) ball Bright green 4 ply (fingering) for Stems and Leaves
- 1 pair of 4mm (US 6, UK 8) knitting needles
- 2 x 2.25mm (US 1, UK 13) double pointed knitting needles
- Wool Needle for sewing up
- Polyester fiber filling

TENSION
19 sts to 4 in (10cm) measured over pattern on 4mm (US 6, UK 8) knitting needles

Tea Cosy (Make 2 Pieces the Same)
Using 4mm (US 6, UK 8) knitting needles and Cream 8ply (DK) yarn held double, cast on 49 sts.
1st row: *K2, P2, rep from * to last st, K1.
Rep this row until work measures 5½ in (14cm).
Shape Top
Next row: K2, *P3tog, K1, rep from * to last 2sts, K2.
Next row: K2, P2, *K1, P1, Rep from *, to last 2sts, K2.
Next row: K1, *Sl1, K1, paso, rep from, * to last st, K1.
Next row: K1, Purl to last st K1.
Next row: K2tog to last st, K1.
Cast off.

To Make Up
With right sides together join cast off stitches and 1 in (2.5cm) either side of this section using a back stitch or other neat seam. Join the lower edges for 2cm on either side. Darn in all ends. Turn the right side out. Your tea cosy is now ready for embellishment.

Wrap 1: To minimize the hole made by turning in mid row, slip next st purl wise, take yarn to opposite side of work, slip st back on to left hand needle, ready to turn, and work next short row.

Cherries

(Make 9, 8 to be joined together in 4 pairs and 1 for the top of cosy)
Using 2.25mm Double Pointed Knitting Needles and Red 4ply yarn cast on 12sts

1st row: Knit.
2nd row: P10, wrap 1, turn.
3rd row: K8, wrap 1turn.
4th row: P6, wrap 1 turn.
5th row: K4, wrap 1 turn.
6th row: Purl all across.
Repeat these 6 rows a further 4 times. Cast off.

To Make Up

With right sides together sew half the seam closed, running a gathering thread around one end. Turn the right way out. Stuff firmly and then finish closing the seam. To shape the cherry take a length of yarn and secure firmly at one end of the cherry, insert right through the cherry and then take it back through to the other end. Fasten off.

Leaves (Make 3)

Using 2.25mm (US 1, UK 13) double pointed knitting needles and bright green 4 ply (fingering) yarn, cast on 3 sts.
Work and "I" Cord for 6 rows.
Work leaf as follows

1st row: K1, yfwd, K1, yfwd, K1.
2nd and alt rows: K 1, P1to last st, K1.
3rd row: K2, yfwd, K1, yfwd, K2.
5th row: K3, yfwd, K1, yfwd, K3.
7th row: K4, yfwd, K1, yfwd, K4.
9th row: K5, yfwd, K1, yfwd, K5.

11th row: Knit.
13th row: Sl 1, K1, paso, K to last 2 sts, K2tog.
14th row: K1, P to last st, K1
Rep last 2 rows until 3 sts rem,
Next row: Sl 1, K2tog, paso. Fasten off.

Stem

Using 2.25mm (US 1, UK 13) double pointed knitting needles and bright green 4 ply (fingering) yarn, cast on 3 sts.
Work and "I" Cord for 5 or 6cm, fasten off.

To Make Up

Join 2 stems together in pairs one slightly lower down than the other so one cherry will hang lower than the other. Use the spare thread to attach a cherry to the other end.

Attaching the cherries to the top of the cosy

Using the photo for guidance.
The leaves may need a press with a warm iron prior to attaching to the cosy. They will sit better if you do. First stitch the 3 leaves evenly placed in position on top of the cosy. Next sew the single cherry in the center of the cosy top. Now take the 4 pairs of cherries and position them evenly around the leaves. Stitch them in place at the top and then catch in a few extra small stitches along the side of the stems so that they do not move about too much. Darn in any loose ends.

All Buttoned Up

You can choose any color you like to tone in with your tea set or if you are giving it as a gift you can think about a friends favorite color scheme. I bought the buttons in a bulk pack of 200 and although they were the most time consuming thing about making the cosy the result looks pretty amazing, I think it is well worth the time taken to cover the whole cosy. You do need to sew each button on separately so that the cosy retains its stretch. Otherwise when you pop it on over the pot you will have buttons popping off in all directions.

Basic knitting skills

MEASUREMENTS
To fit a 6–8 cup tea pot

MATERIALS
- 2 x 2 oz (50 g) balls of 8 ply, (DK) Pure Wool Pink. (I used Cleckheaton County)
- 1 pair of 4mm (US 6, UK 8) knitting needles
- 2, 3.25mm (US 3, UK 10) double pointed knitting needles
- Wool Needle for sewing up
- Small amount of polyester fiber filling
- Approx. 200, ¾ in (2cm) mixed buttons. (I used 4 shades of pink, cream and white) available on Ebay in a craft pack of 200.
- Polyester sewing cotton and sewing needle

TENSION
19 sts to 4 in (10cm) measured over pattern using 4mm (US 6, UK 8) knitting needles

Tea Cosy (Make 2 pieces the same)
Using 4mm (US 6, UK 8) knitting needles and Pink 8 ply (DK) yarn, cast on 42 sts.
1st row: *P2, K3, rep from * to last 2 sts , P2.
2nd row: *K2, P3, rep from * to last 2 sts, K2.
Rep these 2 rows until work measures 5½ in (14cm) ending with a 2nd row.
Shape Top
Next row: * P2, K3togm Rep from * to last 2 sts, P2. 26 sts
Next row: *K2, P1, rep from * to last 2 sts, K2.
Next row: *P2tog, K1, rep from * to last 2sts, P2tog. 17 sts
Next row: *K1, P1, rep from * to last st, K1.
Next row: P1, * Sl 1, K1, paso, rep from * to end. 9 sts
Next row: P1, P2tog 4 times.
Cast off.

Make another side to match.

To Make Up

Place tea cosy together, right sides facing and switch cast off edge together and extend this seam for another 1¼ in (3.5cm) in each direction. Stitch closed lower edge for ½ in (1.5cm). Darn in any loose ends. Turn the right way out.

Next sew on your buttons. Divide the buttons in half so that you sew an equal amount on both side of the cosy and stitch each button on individually.

Mix up the buttons so that you get a good mix of color across the cosy.

Special instruction

Wrap 1: To minimize the hole made by turning in mid row, slip next st purl wise, take yarn to opposite side of work, slip st back on to left hand needle, ready to turn, and work next short row.

Make a knitted ball for the top.

Using 3.25mm (US 3, UK 10) double pointed knitting needles and Pink 8 ply, cast on 12 sts.

1st row: Knit.
2nd row: P10, wrap 1, turn.
3rd row: K8, wrap 1turn,
4th row: P6, wrap 1 turn,
5th row: K4, wrap 1 turn.
6th row: Purl all across.

Repeat these 6 rows a further 4 times. Cast off.

To Make Up

With right sides together sew half the seam closed, running a gathering thread around one end. Turn the right way out. Stuff firmly and then Finish closing the seam. To shape the ball, take a length of yarn and secure firmly at one end of the ball, insert right through the ball and then take it back through to the other end. Fasten off.

Stitch to the top of the tea cosy.

Apple a Day

This is a beautiful tea cosy. Its simple shapes are quite bold and its bright colors look outstanding against a simple white tea service. A great project for the beginner knitter. You can tackle this with confidence knowing you will achieve an amazing result and the chunky cosy will keep your teapot warm and toasty. A winner all round.

SKILL LEVEL
Intermediate knitting skills

MEASUREMENTS
To Fit a 6–8 cup tea pot

MATERIALS
- 3 x 2 ox (50 g) ball of 8 ply Pure Wool in Red
- *Note – Yarn is used double throughout so you will need to wind off half of the third ball to make a small 4th ball or purchase a fourth ball. I used

Cleckheaton Country. Equivalent (DK)
- Small amount of 8 ply (DK) Green for Leaf
- Small amount of 8 ply (DK Chocolate Brown for stem
- 1 pair of 4mm (US 6, UK 8) knitting needles
- Wool Needle for sewing up
- 2, 4mm (US 6, UK 8) double pointed knitting needles

TENSION
19 sts to 4 in (10cm) measured over pattern using 4mm (US 6, UK 8) knitting needles

Tea Cosy (Make 2 pieces the same)
Using 4mm (US 6, UK 8) knitting needles and 8 ply (DK) yarn held double, cast on 49 sts.
1st row: *K2, P2, rep from * to last st, K1.
Rep this row until work measures 5½ in (14cm).

Shape Top
Next row: K2, *P3tog, K1, rep from * to last 2 sts, K2.
Next row: K2, P2, *K1, P1, Rep from *, to last 2 sts, K2.
Next row: K1, *Sl1, K1, paso, rep from, * to last st, K1.
Next row: K1, Purl to last st K1.
Next row: K2tog to last st, K1.
Cast off.

Leaf
Using 4mm (US 6, UK 8) double pointed knitting needles and green 8 ply (DK) held double, cast on 3 sts.
1st row: * Knit, do not turn work, slide sts to other end of needle and pull yarn firmly behind the work, rep from * until ¨I Cord measure 2cm, proceed as follows:
1st row: K1, yfwd, K1, yfwd, K1. 5 sts

21

2nd and alt rows: Knit.
3rd row: K2, yfwd, K1, yfwd, K2. 7 sts
5th row: K3, yfwd, K1, yfwd, K3. 9 sts
7th row: K4, yfwd, K1, yfwd, K4. 11 sts
9th row: K5, yfwd, K1, yfwd, K5. 13 sts
11th row: Sl 1, K1, paso, K9, K2tog.
13th row: Sl 1, K1, paso, K7, K2tog.
15h row: Sl 1, K1, paso, K5, K2tog.
17th row: Sl 1, K1, paso, K3, K2tog.
19th row: Sl 1, K1, paso, K1, K2tog.
21st row: Sl 1, K2tog, psso fasten off.

To Make Up

With right sides together join cast off stitches and 1 in (2.5cm) either side of this section using a back stitch or other neat seam. Join the lower edges for ¾in (2cm) on either side. Darn in all ends. Turn the right side out. Your tea cosy is now ready for embellishment.

Stem

Using 4mm (US 6, UK 8) double pointed knitting needles and brown 8 ply (DK) held double, cast on 3 sts.
1st row: * Knit, do not turn work, slide sts to other end of needle and pull yarn firmly behind the work," rep from * until "I Cord measure 1¼ in (3cm).
Next row: Sl 1 – K2tog, paso, fasten off.

To Make Up

Stitch the stem in an upright position in the center of the top of the tea cosy using small stitches all around the base. Place the "I Cord" section of the leaf right next to the stem and stitch in place with matching yarn.

Autumn Leaves Tea Cosy

This is a tea cosy for knitters with a little patience. It features a collection of beautiful autumnal hued leaves and kicking up his little heels amongst them a tiny hedgehog. None of the elements are difficult to make, they just take a little patience and time when you are sewing up, however the end result is well worth the effort.

SKILL LEVEL
Advanced knitting skills

MEASUREMENTS
To fit a 6–8 cup tea pot

MATERIALS
- 2 x 2 oz (50 g) balls of beige 8 ply Pure Wool (DK)
- 2 x 2 oz (50 g) balls of milk chocolate 8 ply Pure Wool (DK)
- Small amounts of 8 ply leaf colored yarn. Russet, Olive, Green, Grey etc. Pure Wool (DK)
- Small amount of 8 ply Dark Brown Boucle Wool for Hedgehog
- Small amount (less than 1 oz/25 g) of beige fleck 4 ply for hedgehog face. Pure wool.
- 1 pair of 4mm (US 6, UK 8) knitting needles
- 1 pair of 3mm (UK 11) knitting needles
- 2, 3mm (UK 11) double pointed knitting needles
- 1 pair of 2.25mm (US 1, UK 13) double pointed knitting needles
- 1 pair of 2mm (US 0, UK 14) knitting needles
- Polyester fiber filling for Hedgehog
- Wool needle for sewing up
- Black embroidery cotton for hedgehog eyes
- 3.6mm bead for nose

Tea Cosy (Make 2 pieces the same)
Note – You will make 2 pieces the same.
The pleated fabric is created by the yarn not in use being pulled tightly across on the wrong side. It is important to do this on each row. Carry the yarn on the back of the work and right across to the ends of the work. It may seem a little slow to begin with but you will develop a rhythm.

Using 4mm (US 6, UK 8) knitting needles and Milk Chocolate 8 ply, cast on 98 sts. Work 8 rows garter st. (every row knit).
Begin patt.
1st row: K1MC, K6C, *K7MC, K7C, rep from * to last 7 sts. K6MC, K1C. as you knit pull the yarn not in use very firmly behind, to draw up the pleats.
2nd row: K1C, K6MC, *K7C, K6MC, rep from * to last 7 sts, K6C, K1 MC. Keep yarn to the front in this row and continue to pull the yarn not in use tightly so that pleat remains firm.
These 2 rows form patt. Continue in patt until 48 rows have been worked.
Commence decreases – Right side facing.
1st row: K2togM, K3C, K2togC, *K2togM, K3M,

K2togC, K3C, K2togC, rep from * to last 7 sts, K2togM, K3M, K2togC.

2nd row: K1C, K4M, * K5C, K5M, rep from * to last 5 sts, K4C, K1M.

3rd row: K2togM, K1C, K2togC, * K2togM, K1M, K2togM, K2togC, K1C, K2togC rep from * to last 5 sts, K2togM, K1M, K2togC.

4th row: K1C, K2M, * K3C, K3M, rep from * to last 3 sts, K2C, K1M.

5th row: K2togM, K1C, * K2togM, K1M, K2togC, K1C, rep from * to last 3 sts, K2togM, K1C.

6th row: K1C, K1M, * K2C, K2M, rep from * to last 2 sts, K1C, K1M.

7th row: (K2togM) twice, * K2togC, K2togM, rep from * to last 4 sts, (K2togC) twice.

Break off yarn, thread through rem sts, pull up tightly and fasten off.

Make another piece to match.

To Make Up

Darn in any loose ends. With right sides together, stitch from the center top down each side for approx. 2 in (5cm), be sure to end off very firmly. Join sides together at the bottom edge, stitching up each side for approx. 1¼–1½ in (3–4cm). Turn right side out. Your cosy is now ready for embellishing.

Little Hedgehog
Spike

Using 2mm (US 0, UK 14) and boucle cast on 7 sts.

1st row: *K1, yfwd, rep from * to end. 13 sts

2nd row: Purl.

3rd row: K1, * yfwd , K2 rep from * to end. 19 sts

Next row: Purl.

Rep last 2 rows once. 28st. On second inc row end row with K1. 29 sts

Work a further 18 rows st st.

Next row: K3, (k2tog, K3) x5, K1. 24 sts

Break off boucle yarn and join in beige 4 ply.

Knit 1 row.

Next row: Purl.

Next row: Knit.

Next row: Purl.

Next row: K3, (K2tog, K2) x5, K1. 19 sts

Next row: Purl.

Next row: K2, (K2tog, K1) x5, K1. 14 sts

Next row: Purl.

Next row: Knit.

Next row: Purl.

Next row: Knit.

Break off yarn, thread through rem sts. Pull up tightly and fasten off.

To Make Up

Carefully stitch the under body seam. It may be easier to sew the boucle section with matching thread rather than the thick yarn. Leave a gap for stuffing. Fill firmly with polyester fiber filling, especially the nose. Close the remainder of the seam.

Legs (Make 4)

Using 2, 2.25mm (US 1, UK 13) double pointed knitting needles and beige 4 ply, cast on 1 st.

Next: K, P, K, P, K, all into same st. 5 sts.

1st row: Knit.

2nd row: Purl.

3rd row: Knit.

4th row: Purl.

5th row: Knit, do not turn, *slip second st on right hand needle over first, rep from * until 1 st rem. Fasten off.

To Make Up

Run a gathering thread around the outside of the hedgehog leg and draw up to make a nice rounded shape. Darn in any loose ends. Pin the 4 legs into even position on to the underside of Spikes body. Stitch in position.

Face

Stitch the 3.6mm bead in position on the tip of the nose and work two French knots for eyes using Black embroidery cotton.

Leaves (Make a variety of different colored Autumn leaves)

Knit up a selection of Autumn leaves to adorn the top of your cosy. Fan them out from the center of the top of the cosy and the stitch your little hedgehog on the top of his pile of leaves. You can make as many or as few leaves as you like. Use the photo as a guide).

Using 2, 3mm (UK 11) double pointed knitting needles, and color of choice in 8 ply yarn, cast on 3 sts,

1st row: * Knit, do not turn work, slide sts to other end of needle and pull yarn firmly behind the work, rep from * until "I Cord" measure ¾ in (2cm), proceed as follows –

1st row: K1, yfwd, K1, yfwd, K1.

2nd and alt rows: Knit.
3rd row: K2, yfwd, K1, yfwd, K2.
5th row: K3, yfwd, K1, yfwd, K3.
7th row: K4, yfwd, K1, yfwd, K4
9th row: K5, yfwd, K1, yfwd, K5.
11th row: K6, yfwd, K1, yfwd, K6.
13th row: K7, yfwd, K1, yfwd, K7. 17 sts
15th row: Sl 1, K1, paso, K15, K2tog.
17th row: Sl 1, K1, paso, K13, K2tog.
19th row: Sl 1, K1, paso, K11, K2tog.
21st row: Sl 1, K1, paso, K9, K2tog.
23rd row: Sl 1, K1, paso, K7, K2tog.
25th row: Sl 1, K1, paso, K5, K2tog.
27th row: Sl 1, K1, paso, K3, K2tog.
29th row: Sl 1, K1, paso, K1, K2tog.
31st row: Sl 1, K2tog, paso, fasten off.

Autumn Harvest

This is a tea cosy for every one who loves Autumn hues and quirky knitted fruit and vegetables.

SKILL LEVEL
Advanced knitting skills

MEASUREMENTS
To Fit a 6–8 cup tea pot

MATERIALS
- 3 ½ oz (100 g) of Cascade 220 Superwash, Spiced Pumpkin Shade 8 ply (DK) (any pumpkin color in 8 ply Pure Wool is fine) – Main Color
- 2 oz (50 g) of Rowan Felted Tweed Shade 154 – Contrast Color
- Small amount of Sage green 4 ply (fingering) for leaves and tendrils
- Small amount of Green Kid Silk Haze for tendrils
- Small amount of Pumpkin 4 ply (fingering)
- Small amount of Beige 4 ply (fingering) for Stalk
- 1 pair of 4mm (US 6, UK 8) knitting needles
- 1 set of 4, 3mm (UK 11) double pointed knitting needles
- 1 3mm (UK 11) Crochet Hook
- Wool needle for sewing up
- Polyester fiber filling

CROCHET ABBREVIATIONS
Ch – Chain
DC – Double Crochet
SS – Slip Stitch

TENSION
The pleated fabric is created by the yarn not in use being pulled tightly across on the wrong side. Because you are using the same color you will need to use two balls of the same color to create the pleats. You will need to wind off sufficient yarn to create the second ball or buy an additional ball of yarn and use the extra for another project. It is important to do this on each row. Carry the yarn on the back of the work and right across to the ends of the work. It may seem a little slow to begin with but you will develop a rhythm. Every knitter's tension will vary a bit with these projects.

Tea Cosy (make 2 pieces the same)
Using 4mm (US 6, UK 8) knitting needles and Rowan felted Tweed, cast on 98 sts. Work 8 rows garter st. (every row knit).
Begin patt
1st row: K1C,* K6MC, P1C, P6MC, P1C, rep from * to last st, P1C. as you knit pull the yarn not in use very firmly behind, to draw up the pleats.
2nd row: P1C, * K6MC, P1C, P6MC, P1C, rep from * to last st, K1C.
These 2 rows form patt. Continue in patt until 48 rows have been worked.
Commence decreases – Right side facing

1st row: K1, *K2togMC, K2MC, K2MCtog, P1C, P2tog MC, P2MC, P2togMC, rep from *to last st, P1C.

2nd row: K1C, *K4MC, K1C, P4MC, K1C, rep from * to last st K1C.

3rd row: P1C, *K1MC, K2togMC, K1MC, P1C, P1MC, P2togMC, P1MC, P!C, rep from * to last st, P1C.

4th row: K1C, *K3MC, K1C, P3MC, K1C, rep from * to last st, K1C.

5th row: P1C, *K1MC, K2togMC, P1C, P1MC, P2togMC, P1C, rep from * to last st P1C.

6th row: K1C, *K2MC, K1C, P2MC, K1C, rep from * to last st, K1C.

7th row: P1C, *K2togMC, P1C, P2togMC, P1C, rep from * to last st P1.

Break off yarn, thread through rem sts, pull up tightly and fasten off.

Make another piece to match.

To Make Up

Darn in any loose ends. With right sides together, stitch from the center top down each side for approx. 2 in (5cm). Be sure to end off very firmly. Join sides together at the bottom edge, stitching up each side for approx. 1¼–1½ in (3–4cm). Turn right side out. Your cosy is now ready for embellishing.

Pumpkins (Make 4)

Using 3mm (UK 11) double pointed knitting needles and 4 ply pumpkin (fingering yarn), cast on 30 sts. Join into a ring being careful not to twist sts. 10,10,10

1st round: *K2, P1, rep from * to end.

2nd round: K1,* m1, K1, P1, Rep from * to end of round. 40 sts

3rd round: K1, *m1, K2, P1, rep from * to end of round. 50 sts

4th round: *K4, P1, rep from * to end of round. Rep this round fro approx 4 in (10cm).

Next round: *K1, K2tog, K1, P1, rep from * to end of round. 40 sts.

Next round: *K2tog, K1, P1, rep from * to end of round. 30 sts

Break off pumpkin and join in beige. Knit 2 rounds with beige.

To Make Up

Place stitches on to a long length of yarn. Run a gathering thread around the bottom of the pumpkin and draw it in firmly. Stuff the pumpkin well to make a good squashy little shape. Before closing the top. Make your "I Cord" Stem with Beige 4 ply (fingering).

Cast on 5 sts on to 3mm (UK 11) double pointed knitting needle and make a ¾in (2cm) long "I Cord". Secure the "I Cord into the top of the pumpkin and draw closed the top edge. Push needle through from the top to the bottom to give your pumpkin a good authentic shape.

Make 2 more pumpkins.

Leaves (Make 4 using Sage Green 4ply (fingering))

Using 2, 3mm (UK 11) double pointed knitting needles and sage green 4ply, (fingering), cast on 2 sts.

1st row: K2, turn and cast on 1 st.

2nd row: K3, turn and cast on 1 st.

3rd row: K4, turn and cast on 1 st.

4th row: K5, turn and cast on 1 st.

5th row: Knit 6.

6th row: K6, turn and cast on 2 sts.

7th row: K8 turn and cast on 2 sts.

8th row: K10.

9th row: K10.

10th row: K2tog, K6, K2tog.

11th row: K2tog, K4, K2tog.

12th row: K2tog, K2 K2tog.

13th row: K2tog, K1, K2tog. do not turn, make an "I Cord" stem for approx. ¾in (2cm).

K3tog. Fasten off.

Attach 2 leaves to the base of the pumpkins stems. Stitch the remaining leaves to the top of the tea cosy and then sew the pumpkins on top of the leaves in little clusters.

Tendrils

To make the tendrils, crochet a length of chain using a 3mm (UK 11) crochet hook and either sage green 4 ply or green Kid Silk Haze. Work 2dc in to each chain stitch. This creates the curl. Make a total of 6 tendrils in varying lengths. You will need to make at least 50 ch sts to create a reasonable length tendril. Stitch the tendril on to the top of the tea cosy prior to attaching the pumpkins.

Darn in all loose ends.

Basket of Roses Tea Cosy

This tea cosy is perfect for an afternoon tea as it looks like a basket of roses. The roses don't need to be red. Choose your favorite color or one to match your tea set.

The cosy is a simple basket weave stitch which knits up quickly as the yarn is used double, having the added advantage of keeping your tea pot nice and hot.

SKILL LEVEL
Intermediate knitting skills

MEASUREMENTS
To fit a 6–8 cup tea pot

MATERIALS
- 2 x 2 oz (50 g) balls 8 Ply Pure Wool in Beige (DK)
- 2 x 2 oz (50 g) balls 8 Ply Pure Wool in Tweed, (DK)
- 1 x 2 oz (50 g) ball 8 ply Pure Wool in Red (DK)
- 1 x 2 oz (50 g) ball 8 ply Pure Wool in Dark Green (DK)
- 1 pair of 4mm (US 6, UK 8) knitting needles
- Wool needle for sewing up

TENSION
18 sts to 4½ in (10cm) worked over pattern on 4mm (US 6, UK 8) knitting needles

Basket Weave Pattern
1st row: Knit.
2nd row: Purl.
3rd row: K2, *P4, K2, rep from * to end.
4th row: P2, * K4, rep from * to end.
Rep the last 2 rows once more.
7th row: Knit.
8th row: Purl.
9th row: P3, *K2, P4, rep from * to last 5 sts, K2, P3.
10th row: K3, * P2, K4, rep from * to last 5 sts, P2, K3
Rep the last 2 rows once.
These 12 rows form patt.

Tea Cosy
(* sides are worked separately until top shaping then placed together on the same needles and top shaping worked)

Using 4mm (US 6, UK 8) knitting needles and Beige and Tweed yarn held together, cast on 45 sts.
Work 6 rows garter st. (every row knit).
Work 4 repeats of the basket weave pattern.
Shape Top
Next row: *P2, P2tog, rep from * to last st P1. 34 sts
Leave sts on a spare needle.
Work other side to match.
Join Sections
Knit across first set of stitches, Knit together last st on first needle together with first st on spare needle, knit to end. 67 sts

Next row: P2, P2tog, rep from * to last st, P1. 52 sts
Next row: Knit.
Next row: *P1, P2tog, rep from * to end. 34 sts
Next row: Knit.
Next row: * P1, P2tog, rep from * to last st, K1.
   23 sts
Next row: *K1, K2tog, rep from * to end.
Next row: Purl.
Next row: *Sl 1, K1, paso, rep from * to end. 6 sts
Cast off.

To Make Up

With right sides together stitch top seam, leaving an opening for the handle and spout. Stitch closed lower edge for 1¼ in (3cm). Darn in all loose ends. Turn the right way out.

Roses (Make 8)

Using 4mm (US 6, UK 8) knitting needles and Red 8 ply, cast on 34 sts.
Work 2 rows st st, continuing in st st.
Sl 1, K1, paso at the beginning of next and following 4 alt rows.
Cast off leaving a long length of yarn for sewing up.

Leaf Base

The leaf is knitted in one piece and wraps around the rosebud.
Using 4mm (US 6, UK 8) knitting needles and Green 8 ply cast on 21 sts.
1st row: K7, turn (work on these 7 sts for first leaf)
St st 5 rows beg with a purl row.

Dec at each end of next and every row until there are 3 sts rem, ending with a purl row.
Next row: K2tog, K1.
Next row: P2tog.
Fasten off.

Attach yarn to the next 7 sts left on needle and work as before and then do the same again with the remaining 7 sts.

To make up the Rosebud

Press lightly first – This makes it much easier to sew together. With the longest edge at the bottom, start by curling the side in and then sewing it in place from the bottom to half way up the flower. Next sew a gathering thread along the bottom edge and pull in to gather. Start curling the rosebud from the inside edge, the gathering prevents the rosebud looking like a tube. Stitch the rounds in place as you go. Try to keep the bottom flat.

The leaves

Run a gathering thread along the bottom of the leaf piece, just enough to gather it around your rosebud. Stitch in place to secure.

Arrange your Rosebuds on the top of the cosy with the buds facing outwards. It is often easier to sit it on the tea pot when you are doing this part. When you are happy with the arrangement, stitch in place.

Beaker the Baby Blue Owl Tea Cosy

For all owl lovers here is a little baby owl tea cosy. He is half asleep but still keeping an eye on the cake with his button eye. Two wooden buttons adorn his fluffy tummy which is knitted in a mixture of Angora and 8 ply to simulate his downy feathers. When sitting on the tea pot he looks very cuddly.

SKILL LEVEL
Intermediate knitting skills

MEASUREMENTS
To fit a 6–8 cup tea pot

MATERIALS
- 1 x 2 oz (50 g) ball Bright Blue 8ply (DK) Pure Wool (MC – Main Color)
- 1 x 2 oz (50 g) ball Navy 8ply (DK) Pure Wool (MC – Main Color)
- 1 x 2 oz (50 g) ball Biscuit 8ply (DK) Pure Wool (C – Contrast)
- 1 x 1 oz (25 g) ball of Plymouth Angora (or similar light weight fluffy DK yarn) (C – Contrast)
- Small amount of Purple 8 ply (DK) Pure Wool
- 1 x 4 in (10cm) square of White felt
- 1 x 4 in (10 cm) Square of Purple Felt
- 1 x ¾ in (2cm) diameter button for eye
- 2 x 1¼ in (3cm) diameter button for tummy
- Light purple embroidery cotton
- 1 pair of 4.5mm (US 7, UK 7) knitting needles
- 1 pair of 3mm (UK 11) knitting needles
- Wool needle for sewing up
- Sewing needle for the embroidery and attaching buttons

TENSION
18 sts and 26 rows to 4 in (10cm) of stocking st worked on 4.5mm (US 7, UK 7) knitting needles

Eyes
Cut out 2, 1½ in (4cm) diameter White felt circles for outer eye and 2, 1¼ in (3cm) diameter purple circles for inner eyes.

On one eye stitch your ¾ in (2cm) button, sewing securely through both layers of felt and ensuring button is centered. On the other eye mark a curved shape like a smile and embroider this with 6 strands of embroidery cotton in stem stitch.

Next – Blanket stitch around the inner eye to secure it to the outer eye. Set both eyes aside until your back , front and beak have been knitted.

Baby Owl Front
*Note because the tummy section is knitted in and you don't want to be stranding yarn across 19 sts, wind a small ball of both blue shades so that you have blues on one side, Angora and biscuit in the middle and blues again on the other side.
Using 4.5mm (US 7, UK 7) knitting needles and

Bright blue and Navy together, cast on 31 sts.

1st row: Knit.

2nd row: Inc in first three sts, Knit to last 3 sts, inc in last 3sts. 37 sts.

3rd row: Purl.

4th row: K108MC, K17C, K10MC. At the point where colors change always twist the yarns around each other so that you do not have a hole in your work

5th row: P9MC, P19C, P9MC.

6th row: K8MC, K21C, K8MC.

7th row: P8MC, P21C, P8MC

Repeat the last 2 rows a further 9 times

Next row: K9MC, K19C, K9MC.

Next row: P8MC, P21C, P8MC.

Break off tummy colors and continue in blues only.

Next row: (K4, K2tog)3 times, K1, (K2tog, K4)3 times. 31 sts

Next row: Purl.

Next row: K3 K2tog) 3 times, K1, (K2tog, K3)3 times. 25 sts

Commencing with a Purl row work a further 12 rows st st without further shaping.

Cast off.

Baby Owl Back

Using 4.5mm (US 7, UK 7) knitting needles and Bright blue and Navy together, cast on 31sts.

1st row: Knit

2nd row: Inc in first three sts, Knit to last 3sts, inc in last 3 sts. 37 sts.

Beginning with a purl row work a further 25 rows st st.

Next row: (K4, K2tog) 3 times, K1, (K2tog, K4) 3 times. 31 sts.

Next row: Purl.

Next row: (K3 K2tog) 3 times, K1, (K2tog, K3) 3 times. 25 sts.

Commencing with a Purl row work a further 12 rows st st without further shaping.

Cast off.

Beak

Using 3mm (UK 11) knitting needles and Purple 8 ply held double, cast on 2 sts.

1st row: Inc in each st. 4 sts

Next row: Inc in first and last st. 6 sts.

Repeat this last row until there are 12 sts.

Next row: Knit.

Next row: Sl1, K1, psso, K to last 2sts, K2tog. 10 sts.

Repeat the last 2 rows until 4 sts rem.

Next row: K2tog twice.

Next row: K2tog, break off yarn, thread through rem st, pull up tightly and fasten off.

To Make Up

Looking at the photo for guidance you will notice that the top part of Beaker's head is rolled to the front, this gives his owl ears more definition. The cast off edge naturally rolls to the outside so just catch the central section of this rolled edge in place with some small firm stitches. This section should be approx. 3 in (8cm) in length. Place the point of the beak in the center of the top of the tummy section and stitch carefully in place all round. Pin the eyes in place each side. They will overlap the beak slightly. With one strand of embroidery cotton straight stitch all round 2mm from the edge of the outer eye.

Sew the two 1¼ in (3cm) diameter buttons evenly placed on the tummy.

With right sides together sew the top of the cosy together leaving the rolled section open. Stitch down ¾ in (2cm) each side for the ears and lower edge for approx. ¾– 1¼ in (2–3cm) depending upon your tea pot. Darn in all ends and turn the cosy the right way out. Finally stitch together the rolled section at the top of the cosy and press out the ears.

Beautiful Bees Tea Cosy

There are a quite a few beehive tea cosies around so I thought I would make a variation. I have embroidered some lovely bullion bees sitting on a clematis style flower. The honeycomb stitch of the cosy gives a nod to the busy life of the bees.

SKILL LEVEL
Intermediate knitting skills

MEASUREMENTS
To fit a 6–8 cup tea pot

MATERIALS
- 2 x 2 oz (50 g) balls, 8 ply Pure Wool (DK) Yellow yarn (I used Cleckheaton Country)
- Small amount of 8 ply Cream 8 ply Pure Wool (DK)
- Small amount of 8 ply Bright Blue 8 ply Pure Wool (DK)
- Small amount of 8 ply Bright Green 8 ply Pure Wool (DK)
- Yellow, Black and White embroidery cotton
- 1 pair of 4mm (US 6, UK 8) knitting needles
- 2, 3.75mm (US 5, UK 9) double pointed knitting needles
- Embroidery needle
- Wool needle for sewing up

TENSION
20 sts to 4 in (10cm) measured over Honeycomb pattern on 4mm (US 6, UK 8) knitting needles

Flower Petals (Make 6)
Using 4mm (US 6, UK 8) knitting needles and Cream 8 ply, cast on 8 sts.
1st row: K2tog, K4, inc, K1.
2nd row: Knit.
Repeat first and second rows 3 times then first row again. Cast off knit wise.

Center
Using 4mm (US 6, UK 8) knitting needles and bright blue 8 ply yarn cast on 12 sts. Make a loop on each st, K1 but do not slip st from needle; bring yarn forward between needles, take it clockwise around left thumb and back between needles, knit st on left hand needle again slipping it off in the usual way; on right hand needle slip 2nd st over st just made. Cast off, working K2tog across the row.

To Make Up
Leaving the center open, join the petal to half way along inner edges. Pinch a tuck at the inner corner of each petal and stitch. Join ends of center to make a ring and stitch it closed. Set center on petals and stitch in place.

Embroider Bees
The Bees are made from 3 strands of embroidery cotton and bullion knots as follows:
Start with Yellow and a row of 8 bullion knots,

leave a little gap then work a row of 10 knots, then 11 knots, then 8 knots. Fill in the gaps with black bullion knots rows as follows. 9 knot row, 11 knot row, 9 knot row. Work 2 French knots for the eyes. Using 3 strand of White embroidery cotton work 2 lazy daisy stitches on each side for the wings. Work 1 bee on the end of one petal and the other bee on the petal diagonally across.

Leaf

Using 2, 3.75mm (US 5, UK 9) double pointed knitting needles, and Green 8 ply, cast on 3 sts.

1st row: * Knit, do not turn work, slide sts to other end of needle and pull yarn firmly behind the work, rep from * until ¨I Cord measure ¾in (2cm), proceed as follows:

1st row: K1, yfwd, K1, yfwd, K1.

2nd and alt rows: Knit.

3rd row: K2, yfwd, K1, yfwd, K2.

5th row: K3, yfwd, K1, yfwd, K3.

7th row: K4, yfwd, K1, yfwd, K4

9th row: K5, yfwd, K1, yfwd, K5.

11th row: K6, yfwd, K1, yfwd, K6.

13th row: K7, yfwd, K1, yfwd, K7. 17 sts

15th row: Sl 1, K1, paso, K15, K2tog.

17th row: Sl 1, K1, paso, K13, K2tog.

19th row: Sl 1, K1, paso, K11, K2tog.

21st row: Sl 1, K1, paso, K9, K2tog.

23rd row: Sl 1, K1, paso, K7, K2tog.

25th row: Sl 1, K1, paso, K5, K2tog.

27th row: Sl 1, K1, paso, K3, K2tog.

29th row: Sl 1, K1, paso, K1, K2tog.

31st row: Sl 1, K2tog, paso, fasten off.

Tea Cosy

* Note – sides are worked separately to the point where top shaping begins and then placed on one needle and top shaping is worked as one Using 4mm (US 6, UK 8) knitting needles and Yellow 8 Ply, cast on 50 sts.

Work 8 rows Garter St, (every row knit)

Commence Honeycomb pattern

1st row (right side): Purl.

2nd row: Knit.

3rd row: K1, *K1, slip 2 purlwise, (yarn at back), K1* repeat from * to * last st, K1.

4th row: K1, *P1, *slip 2 purlwise (yarn in front), P1*, repeat from * to * to last st, K1.

5th row: K1, *K1, slip 2 purlwise, (yarn at back), K1* repeat from * to * last st, K1.

6th row: K1, *P1, *slip 2 purlwise (yarn in front), P1*, repeat from * to * to last st, K1.

7th row: K1, *K1, slip 2 purlwise, (yarn at back), K1* repeat from * to * last st, K1.

8th row: K1, *P1, *slip 2 purlwise (yarn in front), P1*, repeat from * to * to last st, K1.

9th row: Purl.

10th row: Knit.

11th row: K1, *slip 1 purlwise, (yarn in back), K2, slip 1 purlwise (yarn in back) * repeat from * to * to last st, K1.

12th row: K1, *Sl 1 purlwise (yarn in front), P2, slip 1 purlwise (yarn in front) * repeat from * to * to last st, K1.

13th row: K1, *slip 1 purlwise, (yarn in back), K2, slip 1 purlwise (yarn in back) * repeat from * to * to last st, K1.

14th row: K1, *Sl 1 purlwise (yarn in front), P2, slip 1 purlwise (yarn in front) * repeat from * to * to last st, K1.

15th row: K1, *slip 1 purlwise, (yarn in back), K2, slip 1 purlwise (yarn in back) * repeat from * to * to last st, K1.

16th row: K1, *Sl 1 purlwise (yarn in front), P2, slip 1 purlwise (yarn in front) * repeat from * to * to last st, K1.

These 16 rows form pattern.

Work 5 repeats of the pattern or until work measures 5½ in (14cm) from cast on edge ending with a wrong side row.

Next row: *K2, K2tog, rep from * to last 2 sts. 38 sts leave sts on a spare needle.

Work other side to match.

Slip sts on spare needle on to same needle as just completed side. You will have to break yarn at begin at start of next row otherwise you will end up with an extra half row of knitting on one side.

Next row: Knit.

Next row: *K1, K2tog, rep from * to end. 51 sts

Next row: Knit.

Rep last 2 rows. 34 sts

Next row: *K1, K2tog to last 2 sts, K2. 23 sts

Next row: Knit.

Next row: K1*(K2tog) 11 times.

Next row: (K2tog) 6 times.

Cast off.

To Make Up

With right sides together join cast off stitches and stitch top section together for a further 2 in (5cm) on each side. Stitch garter stitch section together on each side. Turn the right way out. Sew the flower to the center of the top of the cosy. Stitch the stem of the leaf under one of the petals of the flower on the top of the cosy. Darn in any loose ends.

Blue and White Snowballs Tea Cosy

This simple tea cosy goes perfectly with a white china tea set as it looks extremely fresh and spring like. It is a smaller tea cosy and is a great one to try if you are a less advanced knitter or would like a quick project.

SKILL LEVEL
Basic knitting skills

MEASUREMENTS
To fit a 2–3 cup tea pot

MATERIALS
- 1 x 2 oz (50 g) ball 8 ply Pure wool bright blue
- 1 x 2 oz (50 g) ball 8 ply Pure wool cream or white
- *** Note** – Yarn is used double throughout, except for snowballs so you will need to wind off partial balls or else buy an extra ball and use it for another project in the future.

- 1 pair of 5mm (US 8, UK 6) knitting needles
- 2, 3.75mm (US 5, UK 9) double pointed knitting needles
- Polyester fiber filling
- Wool needle for sewing up

TENSION
16 sts and 23 row to 4 in (10cm) of stocking st using 5mm (US 8, UK 6) knitting needles and yarn doubled

Tea Cosy (Make 2 pieces)
Using 5mm (US 8, UK 6) knitting needles and Bright Blue 8 ply, cast on 30 sts.
Work 4 rows of garter st, (every row knit)
Next: work 17 rows of st st, beg with a knit row work in stripes of 2 rows cream, 2 rows bright blue, beginning with cream.
Work 3 rows of garter st in cream
Next: Work 6 rows of st st in cream.
Shape top (Cream 8 ply)
Next row: *K2, K2tog, rep from * to last 2 sts, K2. 23 sts
Work 5 rows st st, beg with a purl row.
Next row: *K2, K2tog, rep from * to last 3sts, K1, K2tog. 17 sts
Next row: Purl.
Next row: K2tog to last st, K1. 9 sts
Break of yarn, thread through rem sts, pull up tightly and fasten off.
Work other side to match.

To Make Up
With right sides together sew the top of the cosy together leaving an opening for the spout and the handle. Sew the lower edges together for approx. 1¼ in (3cm). Darn in all loose ends and turn the right way out. It is much easier to sew the snow balls on the top of the cosy if it is sitting on the tea pot.

Wrap 1: To minimize the hole made by turning in mid row, slip next st purl wise, take yarn to opposite side of work, slip st back on to left hand needle, ready to turn, and work next short row.

Snow Balls (Make 5, 3 cream and 2 bright blue)
Using 3.75mm (US 5, UK 9) knitting needles and color of choice in 8 ply (DK), cast on 12 sts.
1st row: Knit.
2nd Row: P10, wrap 1, turn.
3rd row: K8, wrap 1turn,
4th row: P6, wrap 1 turn,
5th row: K4, wrap 1 turn.
6th row: Purl all across.
Repeat these 6 rows a further 4 times. Cast off.

To Make Up – Snow Balls
With right sides together sew closed half the seam, running a gathering thread around one end.

Turn the right way out. Stuff firmly and then finish closing the seam. To shape the ball, take a length of yarn and secure firmly at one end of the ball, insert right through the ball and then take it back through to the other end. Fasten off.

To Make Up
Arrange the 5 snowballs on the top of the tea cosy. Look at the photograph for guidance. There will be one in the middle with four circling it. Stitch up from underneath the tea cosy and right through the snowball to secure. Take the yarn back through the snowball and to the underside of the tea cosy and fasten off securely. Make sure your snowballs are attached very firmly. You don't want them dropping off into your tea.

Blue Bubbles Tea Cosy

When I was little we had a big glass ball which my Mother said was a Witches ball. Apparently it had washed up on the beach or so the story went. These Noro bobbles worked on Merino Magic Chunky stocking stitch fabric remind me of the Witches ball. The Chunky Yarn makes for a nice firm knitted fabric which does not need to be lined.

SKILL LEVEL
Intermediate knitting skills

MEASUREMENTS
To fit a 2–3 cup tea pot

MATERIALS
- 1 x 3½ oz (100 g) ball of Heirloom Merino Magic Chunky (14 ply) Teale
- 1 x 3½ oz (100 g) Ball of Noro, Blue Shades
- 1 pair of 4.5mm (US 7, UK 7) knitting needles
- 2, 3.75mm (US 5, UK 9) double pointed knitting needles
- Small amount of polyester fiber filling
- Wool needle for sewing up

SPECIAL ABBREVIATION
MB – Make Bobble: Using Noro – on knit row K,p,k,p, k in to next st, turn, Purl 5, turn, K5, turn P5 turn K5, *sl second st over first st, rep from * until 1 sts rem.
On Purl row – P, k,p,k,p into same st, tun, K5, turn, P5, turn, K5, turn P5 turn K5, *sl second st over first st, rep from * until 1 sts rem. Turn, Purl this stitch and continue on in same direction in row as previously.

TENSION
18 sts to 4 in (10cm) measured over st st fabric on 4.5mm (US 7, UK 7) knitting needles

Tea Cosy (Make 2 pieces the same)
Using 4.5mm (US 7, UK 7) knitting needles and Merino Magic, cast on 35 sts. Work in Garter Stitch (every row knit) for 4 rows.
Work 4 rows st st. Knitting the first 2 sts and last 2 sts on each purl row.
1st patt row: *K4, MB, rep from * to last 5 sts K5.
Work 4 rows st st, keeping garter st border correct on purl rows.
2nd patt row: K2,* P4, MB, rep from *to last 6 sts P4, K2.
Work 4 rows st st, keeping garter st border correct on purl rows.
These 10 rows for part.
Work a further 18 row part.
Shape Top
Using Noro
Next row: *K2, K2tog, repp from * to last st, K1.
Next row: Purl.
Next row: (Merino Magic) – *K1, K2tog, rep from *

to last 2 sts, K2.

Next row: Purl.

Next row: Noro – K2tog all across.

Next row: Purl.

Break off yarn, thread through rem sts, pull up tightly and fasten off.

Make another side to match.

Special instruction

Wrap 1: To minimize the hole made by turning in mid row, slip next st purl wise, take yarn to opposite side of work, slip st back on to left hand needle, ready to turn, and work next short row.

Blue Ball for Top of Cosy

Using 3.75mm (US 5, UK 9) knitting needles and Noro, cast on 12 sts

1st row: Knit.

2nd row: P10, wrap 1, turn.

3rd row: K8, wrap 1turn,

4th row: P6, wrap 1 turn,

5th row: K4, wrap 1 turn.

6th row: Purl all across.

Repeat these 6 rows a further 4 times. Cast off.

To Make Up – Blue Ball

With right sides together sew closed half the seam, running a gathering thread around one end. Turn the right way out. Stuff firmly and then Finish closing the seam. To shape the ball, take a length of yarn and secure firmly at one end of the ball, insert right through the ball and then take it back through to the other end. Fasten off.

To Make Up

With right sides together sew closed the top section of the tea cosy to where the garter stitch edge stops on each side. Sew each lower edge closed for approx. ¾ in (2cm). Darn in all loose ends and turn the cosy the right way out. Carefully attach your knitted blue ball to the center of the top of the cosy using small but firm stitches.

Blueberry Pie Tea Cosy

This tea cosy looks like a baked pie, with a crusty edging and a little decoration of leaves and blueberries. It is a large tea cosy and will easily fit a large tea pot. The yarn is used double throughout so there is no danger of your tea pot getting cold. The pattern knits up quickly but it still looks quite spectacular and would make a great gift.

SKILL LEVEL
Intermediate knitting skills

MEASUREMENTS
To fit a 6–8 cup tea pot

MATERIALS
- 2 x 2 oz (50 g) balls 8 ply Pure Wool Dark Purple (DK) I used Cleckheaton Country
- 2 x 2 oz (50 g) balls 8 ply Pure Wool Biscuit (DK) I used Cleckheaton Country
- Small amount 8 ply Pure Wool Bright Green, less than 25 grams (DK) for leaves
- Small amount, less than 1 oz (25 g) Purple 4 ply for blue berries
- 1 pair of 4mm (US 6, UK 8) knitting needles
- 2, 3.25mm (US 3, UK 10) double pointed knitting needles
- 2, 2.25mm (US 1, UK 13) double pointed knitting needles
- Wool Needle for sewing up

TENSION
Due to the thickness of the knitted fabric it is very difficult to measure your tension with blackberry stitch. However, you want your knitted fabric to be good and firm.

Tea Cosy (Make 2 pieces the same)
Using 4mm (US 6, UK 8) knitting needles and 8 ply Purple yarn double, cast on 49 sts.

1st row: *K2, P2, rep from * to last st, K1.

Rep this row a further 23 times.

Break of Purple 8 ply and join in Biscuit 8 ply double.

Work 4 rows st st.

Next row: Picot row – K1, *yfwd, K2tog, rep from * to end.

Work a further 4 rows st st beg with a purl row.

Next: Make a tuck by folding the picot row to the right side. Use a spare needle to lift the purl ridge from the first row and place it on the needle in front of the first st. Purl this together with the first st. Repeat this all along the row. This creates the pie crust.

Work a further 8 rows st st beginning with a knit row.

Shape Top

1st row: *K2tog, K6, rep from * to end of row.

2nd and alt rows: Purl.

3rd row: *K2tog, K5, rep from * to end of row.

5th row: *K2tog, K4, rep from * to end of row.
7th row: *K2tog, K3, rep from * to end of row.
9th row: *K2tog, K2, rep from * to end of row.
11th row: *K2tog, K1, rep from * to end of row.
13th row: K2tog all across. 6 sts
Cast off.
Make another piece to match.

Leaves (Make 3)

Using Bright Green 8 ply and 3.25 (US 3, UK 10)
double pointed knitting needles, cast on 3sts.
Make an "I Cord" for 5 rows.
1st row: K1, yfwd, K1, ywfd, K1.
Next and alt rows: Knit to center st, P center st, knit
   to end.
3rd row: K2, yfwd, K1, ywfd, K2.
5th row: K3, yfwd, K1, ywfd, K3.
7th row: K4, yfwd, K1, ywfd, K4.
9th row: K5, yfwd, K1, ywfd, K5. 13 sts
10th and 11th rows: Knit.
12th row: Sl 1, K1, psso, K9, K2tog.
13th row and alt rows: Knit.
14th row: Sl 1, K1, psso, K7, K2tog.
16th row: Sl 1, K1, psso, K5 K2tog.
18th row: Sl 1, K1, psso, K3, K2tog.
20th row: Sl 1, K1, psso, K1, K2tog.
22nd row: Sl 1, K2tog, psso. Fasten off.

Blueberries (Make 5)

Using 4 ply Purple yarn and 2.25mm (US 1, UK 13)
double pointed knitting needles, cast on 1st.
Next: K, P, K, P, K all in to same st, Turn, Purl, turn,
Knit, turn, Purl, turn, Knit, turn, Purl, turn, Knit,
*pass the second st on right hand needle over the
first, rep from * until first remains. Fasten off.

To Make Up

Run a gathering stitch around the outside edge of
the blueberry and pull up to form a ball. End off
invisibly. Repeat with the other 5 berries. Set aside
for the top of the cosy.

To Make up the Cosy

With right sides together sew the top together,
leaving an opening for the handle and the spout. It
can be a good idea to measure the pieces on your
cosy before sewing to ensure a good fit. Sew the
lower ends closed for approx. 1¼ in (3cm). Darn in
all ends and turn the right way out. On the top of
the cosy, position the three leaves evenly spaced
and stitch in place. Sew the blueberries in a cluster
right in the center of the leaves.

Bouquet of Roses Tea Cosy

This red and white tea cosy features a collection of beautiful roses and a red ribbon. Perfect for an elegant afternoon tea. The cosy would look equally good knitted in black with which roses and a white ribbon. simple but stylish.

SKILL LEVEL
Intermediate knitting skills

MEASUREMENTS
To fit a 6–8 cup tea pot

MATERIALS
- 3 x 2 oz (50 g) balls Cream Pure Wool 8 Ply (DK) (I used Cleckheaton Country)
- 1 x 2 oz (50 g) ball of Red Pure Wool 8 Ply DK, (I used Cleckheaton Country)
- Small amount of Green Pure Wool 8 Ply (DK) for Leaves
- 1 pair of 4mm (US 6, UK 8) knitting needles
- 2, 3.75mm (US 5, UK 9) double pointed knitting needles
- 75cm of 1cm wide Red ribbon (trim to fit)
- Wool needle

TENSION
18 sts to 4 in (10cm) worked over pattern using yarn doubled and 4mm (US 6, UK 8) knitting needles

Roses (Make 5)
Using 2, 3.75mm (US 5, UK 9) double pointed knitting needles and Red 8 ply, cast on 5 sts.

Small Petals
1st row: Inc in first st, K4. 6 sts
2nd row: P4, inc, P1. 7 sts
3rd row: K7.
4th row: P.
5th row: K1, K2tog, K4. 6 sts
6th row: P3, P2tog, P1, 5 sts, Rep 1st–6th row 3 times, do not break yarn.

Medium petals
1st and 3rd rows: Inc in 1st st, knit to end.
2nd and 4th rows: Purl to last 2 sts inc. P1.
5th and 7th rows: K9.
6th and 8th rows: P9.
9th and 11th rows: K1, K2tog, Knit to end.
10th and 12th rows: Purl to last 3 sts, P2tog, P1, 5 sts, do not break yarn. Repeat 1st to 12th rows twice.

Large petals
1st, 3rd and 5th rows: Inc in 1st st, Knit to end.
2nd, 4th and 6th rows: Purl to last 2 sts. inc, P1.
7th, 9th, and 11th rows: K11.
8th, 10th, and 12th rows: P11.
13th, 15th, and 17th rows: K1, K2tog, Knit to end.
14th, 16th and 18th rows: Purl to last 3 sts, P2tog, P1, 5 sts, repeat 1st to 18th rows twice.
Next row: K1, K2tog, K2.
Next row: P1, P2tog, P1.

Next row: K1, K2tog, K2tog.
Next row: P2tog. Fasten off.

To Make Up

Press each piece lightly. With reverse st st to the outside, roll up loosely from the cast on end. Lightly stitch the straight edges together to form a flat base, and then push up the center. turn back the petals and steam if necessary.

Leaves (Make 4)

Using 3.75mm (US 5, UK 9) double pointed knitting needles and green 8ply (DK) yarn, cast on 3 sts.
Work and "I" Cord for 6 rows.
Work leaf as follows –
1st row: K1, yfwd, K1, yfwd, K1.
2nd and alt rows: K 1, P1to last st, K1.
3rd row: K2, yfwd, K1, yfwd, K2.
5th row: K3, yfwd, K1, yfwd, K3.
7th row: K4 , yfwd, K1, yfwd, K4.
9th row: K5, yfwd, K1, yfwd, K5.
11th row: Knit.
13th row: Sl 1, K1, paso, K to last 2 sts, K2tog.
14th row: K1, P to last st, K1.
Rep last 2 rows until 3 sts rem.
Next row: Sl 1, K2tog, paso. Fasten off.

Tea Cosy (Make 2 Pieces the Same)

Using 4mm (US 6, UK 8) knitting needles and Cream 8 ply (DK) yarn held double, cast on 49 sts.
1st row: *K2, P2, rep from * to last st, K1.
Rep this row until work measures 5½ in (14cm).

Ribbon Holes

Next row: K2, *yrn, P2tog, yrn K2tog, rep from * to last st, P1.
Next row: *K2, P2, rep from * to last st, K1.
Shape Top
Next row: K2, *P3tog, K1, rep from * to last 2 sts, K2.

Next row: K2, P2, *K1, P1, Rep from *, to last 2 sts, K2.
Next row: K1, *Sl1, K1, paso, rep from, * to last st, K1.
Next row: K1, Purl to last st K1.
Next row: K2tog to last st, K1.
Cast off.

To Make Up

With right sides together join cast off stitches and 1 in (2.5cm) either side of this section using a back stitch or other neat seam. Join the lower edges for 1½ in (2cm) on either side. Darn in all ends. Turn the right side out. Your tea cosy is now ready for embellishment. Thread ribbon through holes beginning at front of tea cosy so that you will be able to tie in a bow at the spout end. Arrange leaves in position on top of the tea cosy first with stems facing in towards the center. Stitch along the stem line using the same colored yarn and then sew the rose in position once you have arranged then to your satisfaction. Once again you want the bases of the roses facing in towards the center of the cosy. Ensure the roses are firmly attached as you don't want any dropping into your tea. Tie the ribbon into a bow and trim off any extra long ends.

Christmas Hat Tea Cosy

This tea cosy is perfect for your Christmas festivities. I have made it with a knitted pom-pom but you could make a traditional pom-pom if you desire.

SKILL LEVEL
Basic knitting skills

MEASUREMENTS
To fit a 6–8 cup tea pot

MATERIALS
- 1 x 2 oz (50 g) ball of 8 ply Pure Wool Cream (DK) (I used Cleckheaton Country)
- 2 x 2 oz (50 g) balls of Heirloom Merino Magic 8 ply (DK) Red, Shade 512
- 1 pair of 4mm (US 6, UK 8) knitting needles
- Wool needle for sewing up
- Polyester fiber filling for pom-pom

TENSION

22 sts and 28 rows measured over stocking st on 4mm (US 6, UK 8) knitting needles.
Tension is important so check your tension carefully.
If fewer sts try going down a needle size, if less sts try going up a needle size.

Tea Cosy

Note – sides are worked separately to the point where top shaping begins and then placed on one needle and top shaping is worked as one.

Using 4mm (US 6, UK 8) knitting needles and Cream 8ply, (DK), cast on 54 sts.
Work 18 rows in K1, P1 Rib.
Break off Cream and join in Merino Magic Red 8ply (DK).
Next row: Knit.
Next row: K4, Purl to last 4 sts, K4.
Rep these 2 rows until this section measures 3½ in (9cm) ending with a Purl row.
Next row: Dec 4 sts evenly across row.
Next row: K4, Purl to last 4 sts, K4.
Leave sts on a spare needle.

Work next side to match.
Next row: Knit across first set of stitches and then knit across second set of stitches. 100 sts.
Next row: Purl.
Shape Top
1st row: *K8, K2tog, rep from * to end. 90 sts
Work 3 rows st st beg with a Purl row.
5th row: *K7, K2tog, rep from * to end. 80 sts
Work 3 rows st st beg with a Purl row.
9th row: *K6, K2tog, rep from * to end. 70 sts
Work 3 rows st st beg with a Purl row.
12th row: *K5, K2tog, rep from * to end. 60 sts
Work 3 rows st st beg with a Purl row.
16th row: * K4, K2tog, rep from * to end. 50 sts

Work 3 rows st st beg with a Purl row.

19th row: *K3, K2tog, rep from * to end. 40 sts

Work 3 rows st st beg with a Purl row.

22nd row: *K2,K2tog, rep from * to end. 30 sts

Work 5 rows st st beg with a Purl row.

27th row: *K1, K2tog, rep from * to end. 20 sts

Work 5 rows st st beg with a Purl row.

32nd row: Work 2tog all across.

Work 5 rows st st beg with a Purl row.

37th row: Work 2tog all across.

Break off yarn, thread through rem sts, pull up
tightly and fasten off.

Special instruction

Wrap 1: To minimize the hole made by turning in mid row, slip next st purl wise, take yarn to opposite side of work, slip st back on to left hand needle, ready to turn, and work next short row.

Knitted Pom Pom

Using 4mm (US 6, UK 8) knitting needles and Cream 8 ply, (DK), cast on 12 sts.

1st row: Knit.

2nd row: P10, wrap 1, turn.

3rd row: K8, wrap 1turn,

4th row: P6, wrap 1 turn,

5th row: K4, wrap 1 turn.

6th row: Purl all across.

Repeat these 6 rows a further 4 times. Cast off.

To Make Up – Pom-Pom

With right sides together sew closed half the seam, running a gathering thread around one end. Turn the right way out. Stuff firmly and then Finish closing the seam. To shape the ball, take a length of yarn and secure firmly at one end of the ball, insert right through the ball and then take it back through to the other end. Fasten off.

To Make Up

With right sides together stitch closed the shaped seam of the hat section. Sew closed the ribbed sections and fold in half to the outside. Catch closed so that they don't keep falling open. Darn in all loose ends. Sew the knitted pom-pom to the point and fold the point to one side of the cosy, catching invisibly in place with a few small stitches.

Daisy Chain Tea Cosy

This is a small tea cosy is perfect for an afternoon tea set with a lovely plate of homemade cakes. A great project for using odds and ends of left over 8 ply. It is knitted with yarn doubles so is a quick and easy project.

SKILL LEVEL
Intermediate knitting skills

MEASUREMENTS
To fit a 2–3 cup tea pot

MATERIALS
- 1 x 2 oz (50 g) ball of 8 ply Pure Wool Purple (DK)
- 1 x 2 oz (50 g) ball of 8 ply Pure Wool Bright Pink (DK)
- 1 x 2 oz (50 g) ball of 8 ply Pure Wool Light Pink (DK)
- 1 x 2 oz (50 g) ball of 8 ply Pure Wool Mauve (DK)
- 1 x 2 oz (50 g) ball of 8 ply Pure Wool Cream(DK)
- 1 pair of 5mm (US 8, UK 6) knitting needles
- 1, 3.5mm (US E/4, UK 9) Crochet Hook
- Wool needle for sewing up

TENSION
16 sts and 23 row to 4 in (10cm) of stocking st using 5mm (US 8, UK 6) knitting needles and yarn doubled
*Note – yarn is used double throughout except for flowers so you will need to wind off partial balls before you begin the knitting or alternatively buy two balls of each shade.

Stripe Pattern
3 rows Bright Pink
3 rows Light Pink
3 rows Mauve
3 rows Cream

Tea Cosy (Make 2 pieces)
Using 5mm (US 8, UK 6) knitting needles and Purple 8 ply, cast on 30 sts.
Work 4 rows of garter st, (every row knit).
Work in Stripe pattern for the 15 rows. You will have one complete sequence with one further bright pink stripe.
Next: Work 15 rows of st st, beg with a knit row.
Work 3 rows of garter st. (Purple)
Next: Work 6 rows of st st. (Cream)
Shape top (Cream Only)
Next row: *K2, K2tog, rep from * to last 2 sts, K2.
   23 sts
Work 5 rows st st, beg with a purl row.
Next row: *K2, K2tog, rep from * to last 3 sts, K1, K2tog. 17 sts
Next row: Purl.
Next row: K2tog to last st, K1. 9 sts
Break of yarn, thread through rem sts, pull up tightly and fasten off.
Work other side to match.

To Make Up

With right sides together sew the top of the cosy together leaving an opening for the spout and the handle. Sew the lower edges together for approx. 1¼ in (3cm). Darn in all loose ends and turn the right way out. It is much easier to sew the pea pods on the top of the cosy if it is sitting on the tea pot.

Daisies

(Make 8 Daisies in an assortment of different colors. Make the center one shade and the petals a different shade).

Using 3.5mm (US E/4, UK 9) Crochet Hook and 8 ply, make 6 chain, form into a loop with a sl st. Work 1 ch, then 11 dc into the loop formed. Sl st into 1st dc.

Next: Break off yellow and join in cream 8 ply. Make * 11 ch, sl st into next dc, rep from * until 12 petals have been completed. Fasten off.

To Make Up

Stitch 4 daisies along the garter stitch ridge ⅔ of the way up the tea cosy, just before the cream top. Darn in all loose ends.

Darling Daffodil

I made this tea cosy in the absolute depths of Winter and its cheerful colors are like a burst of Spring cheerfulness. I was slightly dubious about mixing the two shades of blue but now I love the result.

The star of this tea cosy is the Daffodil. It is a glorious deep yellow with an orange trumpet, offset with some tiny orange glass beads just to highlight its beauty even more. The petals and trumpet are knitted on double pointed needles and are double sided so it is beautiful from every angle and in fact would make a lovely brooch or hat ornament. I suggest knitting and making the daffodil up first so it is ready to stitch on to your tea cosy as soon as you have finished it. The daffodil is the most time consuming element in this project but well worth the effort. Every time I look at it I feel happy.

SKILL LEVEL

Advanced knitting skills

MEASUREMENTS

To fit a 6–8 cup tea pot

MATERIALS

- 1 x 3½ oz (100 g) ball of light blue 8 ply pure wool (DK) I used Cascade 220 Superwash
- 1 x 3½ oz (100 g) ball of mid blue 8 ply pure wool (DK) Cascade 220 Superwash
- 1 x 2 oz (50 g) ball of Bright yellow 8 ply (DK) I used Cleckheaton Country
- ½ ball Orange 8 ply (DK) I used Cleckheaton Country
- 1 pair of 4mm (US 6, UK 8) knitting needles
- 1 set of 3.25mm (US 3, UK 10) double pointed knitting needles
- Wool Needle for sewing up
- Orange Maria George Glass Beads
- Polyester Sewing Cotton Orange
- Beading Needle

TENSION

19 sts to 4 in (10cm) measured over pattern on 4mm (US 6, UK 8) knitting needles

Tea Cosy (Make 2 pieces the same)

Using 4mm (US 6, UK 8) knitting needles and 8ply (DK) 2 shades of blue yarn held double, cast on 49 sts.

1st row: *K2, P2, rep from * to last st, K1.

Rep this row until work measures 5½ in (14cm).

Shape Top

Next row: K2, *P3tog, K1, rep from * to last 2sts, K2.

Next row: K2, P2, *K1, P1, Rep from *, to last 2sts, K2.

Next row: K1, *Sl1, K1, paso, rep from, * to last st, K1.

Next row: K1, Purl to last st K1.
Next row: K2tog to last st, K1.
Cast off.

To Make Up

With right sides together join cast off stitches and 1 in (2.5cm) either side of this section using a back stitch or other neat seam. Join the lower edges for ¾in (2cm) on either side. Darn in all ends. Turn the right side out. Your tea cosy is now ready for embellishment.

Daffodil Trumpet (Make one)

Using 3.25mm (US 3, UK 10) double pointed knitting needles and Orange 8 ply yarn, cast on 6sts. 2.2.2. Join into a round being careful not to twist the stitches.

1st round: Knit.

2nd round: Inc, in each st. 12 sts

3rd round: Knit.

4th round: *K3, m1, rep from * to end of round. 16 sts

5th round – 10th round: Knit.

11th round: * K4, m1, rep from * to end of round. 20 sts

12th round: Knit.

13th round: K2, *m1, K5, rep from * to last 3 sts, m1, K3. 24 sts

14th round: Knit.

15th round: Knit.

16th round: *yfwd, k2tog, rep from * to end of round.

17th round: Knit.

18th round: Knit.

19th round: * K4, K2tog, rep from * to end of round. 20 sts

20th round: Knit.

21st round: K1, K2tog, *K3, K2tog, rep from * to last 2 sts. 16 sts

22nd round – 26th round: Knit.

27th round: *K2, K2tog, rep from * to end of round.

28th round: Knit.

29th round: *K2tog, rep from * to end of round.
Break off yarn, thread through rem sts. Pull up tightly and fasten off. Push the top section of the trumpet inside the bottom section and fan out along the picot edge. Take a few stitches through the bottom to hold the two sections firmly together. Using the photo for guidance stitch a row of orange glass beads around the inner edge of the trumpet using orange polyester cotton and the beading needle and then stitch one orange glass bead to each pointed edge of the picot edging. Be sure to fasten off your work very well. You don't want any beads dropping in someone's tea.

Petals (Make six)

Using 3.25mm (US 3, UK 10) double pointed knitting needles and yellow 8 ply (DK), cast on 12 sts. 4,4,4. Join into a ring being careful not to twist the stitches.

This is the lower edge of the petal and will be stitched to the trumpet.

1st round: *K5, P1, rep from * to end.

2nd round: *K2, m1, K1, m1, K2, P1, rep from * to end. 16 sts

3rd round: * K7, P1, rep from * to end.

4th round: * K3, m1, K1, m1, K3, P1, rep from * to end. 20 sts

5th round: *K9, P1, rep from * to end.

6th round: * K4, m1, K1, m1, K4, P1, rep from * to end. 24 sts

7th round: *K11, P1, rep from * to end.

8th round: *Sl 1, K1, paso, K3, m1, K1, m1, K3, K2tog, P1, rep from * to end.

9th round: *K11, P1, rep from * to end.

10th round: *Sl 1, K1, paso, K3, m1, K1, m1, K3, K2tog, P1, rep from * to end.

11th round: *K11, P1, rep from * to end.

12th round: *Sl 1, K1, paso, K7, K2tog, P1, rep from * to end. 20 sts

13th round: *K9, P1, rep from * to end.

14th round: *K9, P1, rep from * to end.

15th round: *Sl 1, K1, paso, K3, K2tog, P1, rep from * to end.

16th round: *K7, P1, rep from * to end.

17th round: * *K7, P1, rep from * to end.

18th round: *Sl 1, K1, paso, K3, K2tog, P1, rep from *to end. 12 sts

19th round: *K5, P1, rep from * to end.

20th round: *K5, P1, rep from * to end.

21st round: * Sl 1, K1, paso, K1, K2tog, P1, rep from * to end. 8 sts

22nd round: *K3, P1, rep from * to end.
Break off yarn thread through rem sts, pull up tightly and fasten off.

To Make up

Place all six petals in a circle with the bases overlapping. Stitch together using small stitches following the line of the knit stitches. You only want to leave a small hole in the center for the trumpet to sit in. By overlapping the petals, it helps the daffodil obtain a more upright shape. Finally stitch the trumpet into the center, using very small stitches. Once your daffodil is complete sew it to the top of your tea rosy. It will look amazing.

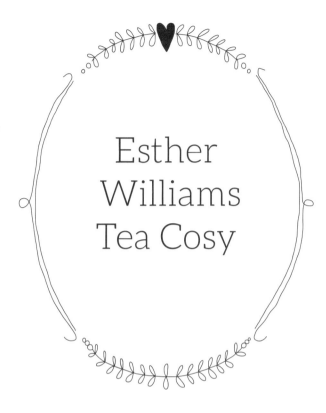

Esther Williams Tea Cosy

This tea cosy is made to look like the bathing caps worn by the graceful swimmers of the Esther Williams period. It is a basic tea cosy adorned with many, many flowers. You will need to make about 45 flowers but the result is just glorious. Choose a shade to match your tea set or just your favorite colors.

SKILL LEVEL
Intermediate knitting skills

MEASUREMENTS
To fit a 6–8 cup tea pot

MATERIALS
• 2 x 2 oz (50 g) balls of 8 Ply Dark Blue (DK)
• Small amount of Mid Blue 8 ply (DK)
• Small amount of Light Blue 8 ply (DK)
• 1 oz (25 g) of 4 ply Bright Blue (fingering)
• 1 oz (25 g) of 4 ply Navy (fingering)
• 1 oz (25 g) of 4 ply Sky Blue (fingering)
• 1 oz (25 g) of 4 ply Yellow (fingering)
• 1 oz (25 g) of 4 ply Provencal Blue (fingering)
• 1 oz (25 g) of 4 ply Purple (fingering)
• 1 pair of 4mm (US 6, UK 8) knitting needles
• 1, 3mm (UK 11) Crochet Hook
• Wool needle for sewing up

TENSION
21 sts to 4 in (10cm) measured over Blackberry Stitch pattern on 4mm (US 6, UK 8) knitting needles

CROCHET ABBREVIATIONS
Ch – Chain
DC – Double Crochet
SS – Slip Stitch

Tea Cosy
Using 4mm (US 6, UK 8) knitting needles and Navy 8 ply, cast on or 54 sts.
Commencing with a knit row work 8 rows st st.
Next row: K1, * yfwd, K2tog, rep from * to last 2 sts, K2.
Commencing with a Purl row work a further 7 (9) rows st st.
Next row: With right side facing, fold up hem at picot edge and knit 1 st together with loop from cast on edge until all sts have been worked off.
Commence Patt.
1st row: Purl.
2nd row: K1, *K1,P1, K1, all into same st, P3tog, rep from * to last st, K1.
3rd row and 5th row: Purl.
4th row: K1, * P3tog, K1, P,1K1 all into same st, rep from * to last st. K1.
Rows 2–5 form patt.
Continue in patt until work measures 6½ in (17cm) from picot edge ending with a 6th patt row.
Commence decrease for top.

Next row: P1, *P1, P3tog, rep from * to end.
Next row: K2tog all across.
Break off yarn thread through rem sts. Pull up
   tightly and fasten off.

To Make Up

With right sides together carefully stitch the top
seam closed, from the center point down, approx.
2–2½ in (5–6cm) each side. Turn the right way out.

Handle and Spout Openings

Using 4mm (US 6, UK 8) knitting needles and mid
blue 8 ply wool, with the right side facing pick up
and knit 55 sts along both pieces. Work 5 rows mid
blue, 2 rows light blue, 5 rows mid blue st st. Cast
off.

To Make up

Fold piece to the wrong side and carefully stitch in
place. You are now ready to join the bottom seam

for approx. 1¼–1½ in (3–4cm).
Darn in any loose ends.
Your tea cosy is now ready to have its adornments
attached.

Flowers (Make 45 in a variety of different shades of blue and yellow)

Using 3mm (UK 11) Crochet Hook and desired color
4 ply make 5 chain, form into a loop with a sl st.
1st round: 3ch, 2-st tr cluster, 2ch. [3-st tr cluster,
   2ch] 4 times, with yarn B, ss to top of 3ch. 5
   cluster and 5 ch sp. Continue with B.
2nd round: [5dc in ch sp] 5 times with C ss to first
   dc 25 sts. Continue with C.
3rd round: [Ss in next dc] 5 times, ss to first ss.
   Fasten off invisibly.

To Make Up

Darn in all ends and stitch the flowers all over the
cosy so it it is covered entirely with flowers.

66

Giant Pink Daisy Tea Cosy

Orange and Pink make a great combination and topped topped with a hot pink Angora daisy made with an "I Cord" this is an eye catching tea cosy.

SKILL LEVEL
Basic knitting skills

MEASUREMENTS
To fit a 6–8 cup tea pot

MATERIALS
- 2 x 2 oz (50 g) balls of 8 ply Pure wool Orange (DK)
- 1 x 1 oz (25 g) ball Rowan Angora Haze in Hot Pink (equivalent to a fluffy fingering weight)
- 1 pair of 4.5mm (US 7, UK 7) knitting needles
- 2, 3.25mm (US 3, UK 10) double pointed knitting needles
- 2, 2.25mm (US 1, UK 13) double pointed knitting needles
- Small amount of polyester fiber filling
- Wool needle for sewing up

TENSION
16 sts and 22 rows to 4 in (10cm) worked over pattern on 4.5mm (US 7, UK 7) knitting needles

Tea Cosy (Make 2 pieces the same)
Note – Yarn is used double throughout for the tea cosy and "I Cord" Daisy.
Using 4.5mm (US 7, UK 7) knitting needles and Orange 8 ply held double, cast on 42 sts.
1st row: *P2, K3, rep from * to last 2 sts P2.
2nd row: *K2, P3, rep from * to last 2 sts, K2.
Rep the 2 rows 4 times.
Work 4 rows Rowan Angora Haze garter st (every row knit).
These 14 rows form pattern.
Repeat pattern once more then a further 8 rows orange 8 ply.

Shape Top
1st row: *P2, K3tog, rep from * to last 2sts, P2.
26 sts
2nd row: K2, P1, rep from * to last 2 sts K2.
3rd row: *P2tog, K1, rep from * to last 2 sts, P2tog.
17 sts
4th row: *K1, P1, rep from * to end of row.
5th row: P1, *, Sl 1, K1, psso, rep from * to end.
9 sts
6th row: P1, P2tog 4 times.
Cast off.
Make another side to match.

To Make Up
With right sides together stitch top together leaving an opening for spout and handle. Stitch lower edges together for approx. 1 in (2.5cm). Darn in all loose ends. Turn the right way out.

"I Cord" Daisy

Using 3.25mm (US 3, UK 10) double pointed knitting needles and yarn double, make an "I Cord" 33½ in (85cm) long.

Cast on 3 sts.

1st row: * Knit.

Do not turn, slide sts to other end of the needle, pull yarn firmly behind the work and repeat the 1st row. Continue in this manner until your "I Cord" is 5½ in (14cm). To finish off. Sl 1 K2tog psso, fasten off.

To Make Up

Take a 6½ in (17cm) section and fold in half, stitch in place to make a loop. This makes the first petal. Take the next 6½ in (17cm) section and make the next petal in the same manner. Stitch through the base of the first petal so that they are anchored together. Repeat until you have a flower with five petals.

Repeat with the pink "I Cord". Place the pink flower on top of the orange flower offsetting the petals so that they do not sit directly on top of each other. Stitch to the top of the tea cosy. This can be easier to do when the cosy is sitting on top of the tea pot. Stitch the knitted button in the center of the flower.

Special instruction

Wrap 1: To minimize the hole made by turning in mid row, slip next st purl wise, take yarn to opposite side of work, slip st back on to left hand needle, ready to turn, and work next short row.

Knitted button

Using 2.25mm (US 1, UK 13) knitting needles and Rowan Angora Haze, (single strand), cast on 12 sts.

1st row: Knit.
2nd row: P10, wrap 1, turn.
3rd row: K8, wrap 1turn.
4th row: P6, wrap 1 turn.
5th row: K4, wrap 1 turn.
6th row: Purl all across.

Repeat these 6 rows a further 4 times. Cast off.

To Make Up

With right sides together sew half the seam closed, running a gathering thread around one end. Turn the right way out. Stuff firmly and then Finish closing the seam. To shape the button, take a length of yarn and secure firmly at one end of the button, insert right through the button and then take it back through to the other end. Fasten off.

Lavender Fair Isle

This is a smaller tea cosy a is a great way to practice your Fair Isle knitting skills and is not too difficult as there are only two colors involved. I have chosen a beautiful dark lavender and cream but don't be put off by this if purple is not a favorite. Choose two of your favorite colors. Cream is always a good blending color but two bright colors can also work well together. Remember when knitting with two colors, always carry the color not in use loosely behind the work and if there are more than 8 stitches to be covered before using the second color again, loop the yarn in use around the yarn not in use so that your tension remains stable.

MEASUREMENTS
To fit a 6–8 cup tea pot

MATERIALS
- 2 x 2 oz (50 g) balls of Debbie Bliss Blue Faced Leicester Aran for Lining (Pale Mauve) approx. 10 ply
- 1 x 2 oz (50 g) ball of Almerino Rooster Aran, Cream for Main part, approx 10 ply
- 1 x 2 oz (50 g) ball of Debbie Bliss Blue Faced Leicester Aran for main part (Dark Lavender) approx. 10 ply
- 1 pair of 4.5mm (US 7, UK 7) knitting needles
- Wool needle for sewing up

TENSION
22 sts and 29 rows to 10cm measured over Fair Isle Pattern on 4.5mm (US 7, UK 7) knitting needles

Tea Cosy (Make 2 pieces the same)
*Note – begin the knitting with the lining.
Using 4.5mm (US 7, UK 7) knitting needles and Debbie Bliss Blue Faced Leicester Aran in Pale Mauve, cast on 9 sts.
1st row: Inc into each of first 8 sts, K1. 17 sts.
2nd row: Purl.
3rd row: K1, *inc in next st, K1, rep from * to end of row. 25 sts.
4th row: Purl.
5th row: K1, *inc in next st, K2, rep from * to end of row. 33 sts.
6th, 7th and 8th rows: Stocking st, beg with a Purl row.
9th row: K1, *inc in next st, K3 rep from * to end. 41sts.
Work 40 rows stocking st, beg with a purl row.
Next row: Knit.
Next row: K5, * m1, K6, rep from * to end of row. 47 sts.
Next row: Purl.
Break off Mauve yarn and join in Cream and Dark Lavender yarn for working chart.
Work 38 rows of chart work reading from right to

left on knit rows and left to right on purl rows. When the 38th row of the chart is complete break off Cream yarn and complete the remainder of the cosy in Lavender only.

Shape Top
Next row: K2, (K2tog, K3) 9 times. 38 sts.
Next row: Purl.
Next row: Knit.
Next row: P2tog, (P1, P2tog)12 times. 25 sts.
Next row: Knit.
Next row: P2, (P2, P2tog) 6 times.
Next row: Knit.
Next row: P2, (P3tog, P3) twice, P3tog, P2. 13 sts.

Next row: K2tog, (K1, K3tog) twice, K1, K2tog. 7 sts. Cast off.
Make Another side to match.

To Make Up
Join top layers along cast off edge and sides to fold line, leaving openings at each side for the spout and handle. Next join lining together leaving opening to match the top layer. Push the lining inside the top layer then join top layer and linings together on each side of the openings using small slip stitches. Press lightly using a warm iron and a damp cloth if needed. Darn in any loose ends.

Number	Name	Strands	Estimated Lenght
Ecru	(Ecru)	2	136.1 in.
DMC 3838	Lavender Blue DK	2	170.1 in.

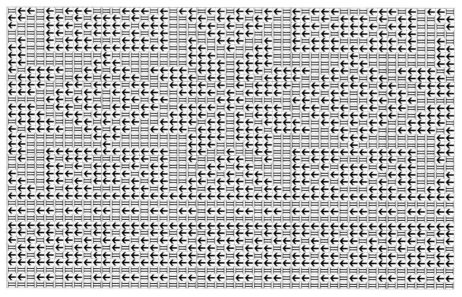

Lemon Tea, Tea Cosy

This stunning tea cosy would make a great gift for the herbal tea drinkers. It features a beautiful knitted lemon, a lemon blossom flower and three large citrus leaves to balance the design. The cosy is knitted in a mix of orange and yellow 8ply and will fit a large tea pot.

SKILL LEVEL
Intermediate knitting skills

MEASUREMENTS
To fit a 6–8 cup tea pot

MATERIALS
- 2 x 2 oz (50 g), 8 ply Pure Wool Yellow (DK)
- 2 x 2 oz (50 g), 8 ply Pure Wool Orange (DK)
- *Note – you will not need the full two balls, some of remainder of yellow will be used for the lemon and lemon blossom

- Small amount of 8 ply pure wool cream (DK)
- Small amount (less than 1 oz/25 g) 8 ply bright green for leaves (DK)
- 1 pair of 4mm (US 6, UK 8) knitting needles
- Set of 4, 3.25mm (US 3, UK 10) double pointed knitting needles
- 2, 3.75mm (US 5, UK 9) double pointed knitting needles
- Wool needle for sewing up
- Polyester fiber filling for Lemon

TENSION
18 sts to 4 in (10cm) worked over part on 4mm (US 6, UK 8) knitting needles

Lemon (Make 1)
Using 2, 3.25mm (US 3, UK 10) double pointed knitting needles and yellow 8 ply, cast on 3 sts.

1st row: Inc in st 2 sts. 5 sts

2nd row: Purl.

3rd row: K1, [m1, K1] 4 times. 9 sts. Slip 3 sts on to each of 3 double point knitting needles and continue in rounds.

1st round: Knit.

2nd round: *K1, (m1, K1) twice, repeat from * twice. 15 sts

3rd round: Knit.

4th round: *K1, (m1, K1)4 times, repeat from * twice. 27 sts

5th, 6th and 7th rounds: st st.

8th round: * K2, m1, K5, m1, K2, repeat from * twice. 33 sts

9th, 10th and 11th rounds: st st.

12th round: *K3, m1, K5, m1, K3, repeat from * twice. 39 sts

13th, 14th, 15th, 16th ,17th, 18th, 19th, and 20th rounds: st st.

21st round: *K2, K2tog, K5, K2tog, K2, repeat from * twice. 33 sts

22nd, 23rd and 24th rounds: st st.

25th round: *K2, K2tog, K3, K2tog, K2, rep from * twice. 27 sts

26th, 27th and 28th rounds: st st.

29th round: *K1, K2tog, 4times, repeat from * twice. 15 sts

30th round: Purl.

Insert stuffing at this point – Stuff firmly and ensure that the filling goes right to the tip.

31st round: * K1, K2tog, twice, repeat from * twice. 9 sts

32nd round: Purl.

33rd round: *K1, K2tog, rep from * twice. 6 sts

34th round: K2tog 3 times.

Break off yarn, thread through rem sts pull up tightly and fasten off.

Lemon Blossom (Make 1)

Use Cream 8 ply for the outer petals and yellow 8 ply (DK) for the center.

Using 2, 3.25mm (US 3, UK 10) double pointed knitting needles and Cream 8 ply (DK), cast on 4 sts.

1st row: K4.

2nd row: (K1, P1, K1, P1, K1) in first st) turn, K5, turn, P5, turn, K5, turn, P2tog twice, P1, take yarn back and on right hand needle slip 2nd and 3rd sts over 1st to complete petal, * P2, turn, slip 1, K2.

3rd row: P4

Repeat 1st to 3rd rows 3 times and then work 1st and 2nd rows to *. Cast off purl wise.

To Make Up

With st st side to the outside, join cast on and cast off edges. Slightly gather the center. Using yellow 8 ply, stitch a ring of small loops around the center, catching each in place with a back stitch on the wrong side. Cut the loops and fluff them out, trimming if needed.

Leaves (Make 3)

Using 3.75mm (US 5, UK 9) double pointed knitting needles and bright green 8 ply (DK), cast on 3 sts.

1st row: * Knit, do not turn work, slide sts to other end of needle and pull yarn firmly behind the work, rep from * until "I Cord" measures ½ in (1.5cm), proceed as follows:

1st row: K1, yfwd, K1, yfwd, K1. 5 sts

2nd and alt rows: Knit.

3rd row: K2, yfwd, K1, yfwd, K2. 7 sts

5th row: K3, yfwd, K1, yfwd, K3. 9 sts

7th row: K4, yfwd, K1, yfwd, K4. 11 sts

9th row: K5, yfwd, K1, yfwd, K5. 13 sts

11th row: K6, yfwd, K1, yfwd, K6. 15 sts

13th row: K7, yfwd, K1, yfwd, K7. 17 sts

15th row: Knit.

16th and WS rows: Knit.

17th row: Sl 1, K1, psso, K13, K2tog. 15 sts.

19th row: Sl 1, K1, psso, K11, K2tog. 13 sts.

21st row: Sl 1, K1, psso, K9, K2tog. 11 sts.

23rd row: Sl 1, K1, psso, K7, K2tog. 9 sts.

25th row: Sl 1, K1, psso, K5, K2tog. 7 sts.

27th row: Sl 1, K1, psso, K3, K2tog. 5 sts.

29th row: Sl 1, K1, psso, K1, K2tog. 3 sts.

31st row: Sl 1, K2tog, psso, Fasten off.

Tea Cosy (make 2 pieces the same)

Using 4mm (US 6, UK 8) knitting needles and 1 strand of Orange 8 ply (DK) and 1 strand of Yellow 8 ply (DK), held together, cast on 49 sts.

1st row: *K2, P2, rep from * to last st, K1.

Rep this row until work measures 5½ in (14cm).

Shape Top

Next row: K2, *P3tog, K1, rep from * to last 2sts, K2.

Next row: K2, P2, *K1, P1, Rep from *, to last 2sts, K2.

Next row: K1, *Sl1, K1, paso, rep from, * to last st, K1.

Next row: K1, Purl to last st K1.

Next row: K2tog to last st, K1.

Cast off.

To Make Up

With right sides together stitch the top of the cosy together leaving an opening for the spout and the handle. It can be a good idea to try it on the pot at this stage before completely sewing up and pin in place. Stitch lower edges together for approx. 1¼ in (3cm). Darn in all loose ends and turn the right way out.

Sew the lemon blossom to the end of one leaf and then position the leaves evenly around the top of the cosy. Stitch in place down the center of their stems. Position the lemon over the top of the lemon stems and stitch in place coming up from the underside of the cosy so that your stitches are invisible. Make sure your lemon is sitting on very firmly, not wobbling about.

Little Christmas Cosy

A perfect little tea cosy to put on the pot for that first cup of tea on Christmas morning. With oversized holly leaves and a bright red pom-pom it is sure to be a hit.

SKILL LEVEL
Intermediate knitting skills

MEASUREMENTS
To fit a 2–3 cup tea pot

MATERIALS
- 1 x 2 oz (50 g) ball Pure Wool Red 8 ply (DK)
- 1 x 2 oz (50 g) ball Pure Wool Cream 8 ply (DK)
- 1 x 2 oz (50 g) ball Pure Wool Dark Green 8 ply (DK)
- 1 pair of 4.5mm (US 7, UK 7) knitting needles
- 1 pair of 4mm (US 6, UK 8) knitting needles
- Wool needle for sewing up
- Sewing needle
- Polyester fiber filling
- 18, 2 in (5cm) red Swarovski Crystals (for holly berries)

TENSION
15 sts to 4 in (10cm) in width measured over Blackberry Stitch pattern on 4.5mm (US 7, UK 7) knitting needle with yarn double.
*Note – Yarn is used double throughout, except for Holly leaves and pom-pom

Blackberry Stitch Pattern
1st row: Purl.
2nd row: K1, * , (K1, P1, K1) all in to same st, P3tog, rep from * to last st, P1.
3rd and 4th row: Purl.
5th row: K1, *P3tog, (K1, P1, K1) all into same St, rep from * to last st, K1.
Repeat rows 2–5 inclusive.

Tea Cosy (Make 2 pieces the same)
Using 4.5mm (US 7, UK 7) knitting needles and Cream 8ply (DK) held double, cast on 30 sts.
Work 4 rows garter st, (every row knit). Break off cream and join in red (double).
Work in Blackberry Stitch pattern, (see above) until work measures 3½ in (9cm) from beg ending with a purl row. Break off Red and join in Cream 8 ply (DK) held double.
Shape Top
1st row: Purl.
2nd row: Purl.
3rd row: Knit.
4th row: Knit.
5th row: Purl.
6th row: *K2, K2tog, rep from * to last 2sts, K2.
7th row: Purl.
8th row: * K2, K2tog, rep from * to last 3 sts, K1, K2tog.
9th row: Purl.

10th row: K2tog all across.

11th row: Purl.

Break off yarn, thread through rem sts, pull up tightly and fasten off.

Make another piece to match.

Holly Leaves (Make 6)

Using 4mm (US 6, UK 8) knitting needles and dark green 8 ply, cast on 3sts. Work 3 rows garter st. Every row knit.

4th row: K1, yfwd, K1, yfwd, K1. 5 sts

5th row: K1, Purl to last st, K1.

6th row: K2, yfwd, K1, yfwd, K2. 7 sts

7th row: As row 5.

8th row: K3, yfwd, K1, yfwd, K3. 9 sts

9th row: As row 5.

10th row: K4, yfwd, K1, yfwd, K4. 11 sts

11th row: As row 5.

12th row: K5, yfwd, K1, yfwd, K5.

13th row: Cast off 4 sts, purl to last st, K1.

14th row: Cast off 4 sts, K2 (including st already on right hand needle) yfwd, K1, yfwd, K2.

15th row: As row 5.

16th row: As row 8.

17th row: As row 5.

18th row: As row 10. 11 sts

19th row: Cast off 3 sts, Purl to last st, K1.

20th row: Cast off 3 sts, K2 (including st already on right hand needle) yfwd, K1, yfwd, K2.

21st row: As row 5.

22nd row: As row 8.

23rd row: K1, P2, P3tog, P2, K1.

24th row: K2, Sl 1, K2tog, psso, K2.

25th row: K1, P3tog, K1.

26th row: P3tog. Fasten off.

To Make Up

Using polyester seeing cotton, stitch a cluster of 3 Swarovski crystals to each holly leaf. Using the photo for guidance choose a slightly different spot for each cluster.

Sew three holly leaves to each side of the cosy, angling them with the base pointing down and slanting from right to left. It is easier to do this before you completely put the cosy together.

Special instruction

Wrap 1: To minimize the hole made by turning in mid row, slip next st purl wise, take yarn to opposite side of work, slip st back on to left hand needle, ready to turn, and work next short row.

Pom-Pom

Using 4mm (US 6, UK 8) knitting needles and Red 8 ply, (DK).

1st row: Knit.

2nd row: P10, wrap 1, turn.

3rd row: K8, wrap 1, turn.

4th row: P6, wrap 1, turn.

5th row: K4, wrap 1, turn.

6th row: Purl all across.

Repeat these 6 rows a further 4 times. Cast off.

To Make Up – Pom-Pom

With right sides together sew closed half the seam, running a gathering thread around one end. Turn the right way out. Stuff firmly and then Finish closing the seam. To shape the cherry, take a length of yarn and secure firmly at one end of the pom-pom insert right through the pom-pom and then take it back through to the other end. Fasten off.

To Make Up

With right sides together sew the top of the cosy together leaving an opening for the handle and spout. It can be a good idea to try the cosy on the pot prior to sewing so that you can ensure a good fit. Stitch the lower edges closed for approx. ¾ in (2cm). Darn in all loose ends. Turn the right way out. Stitch the red pom-pom to the top of the cosy. Make sure it is securely attached. You don't want it suddenly dropping into your tea.

Little Leaves Tea Cosy

This is a tea cosy for a small tea pot. I think it is always handy to have a few different sized tea cosies about as you don't always want to be making gallons of tea. Although in my case I nearly always do. I have knitted this tea cosy in beautiful Debbie Bliss Blue Faced Leicester Aran which is equivalent to a 10 ply. You could reduce it to an 8 ply or DK yarn if you wanted to and it would come out a little smaller still.

SKILL LEVEL
Intermediate knitting skills

MEASUREMENTS
To fit a 2–3 cup tea pot

MATERIALS
- 1 x 2 oz (50 g) ball Debbie Bliss Blue Faced Leicester Aran, Dark Purple. (10 ply)
- 1 x 2 oz (50 g) ball Debbie Bliss Blue Faced Leicester Aran, Mid Purple. (10 ply)
- 1 x 2 oz (50 g) ball Debbie Bliss Blue Faced Leicester Aran, Mauve. (10 ply)
- 1 pair of 4.5mm (US 7, UK 7) knitting needles
- 2, 3.75mm (US 5, UK 9) double pointed knitting needles
- Wool needle for sewing up

*Note – You won't need all the yarn for this project and can probably make 2 cosies from the 3 balls. A good project for gift making or the school fete.

TENSION
20 sts to 4 in (10cm) measured over pattern on 4.5mm (US 7, UK 7) knitting needles

Tea Cosy (Make 2 pieces the same)
Using 4.5mm (US 7, UK 7) knitting needles and Dark Purple Aran, cast on 31 sts.
Knit one row. Begin pattern as follows;
1st row: (wrong side) K3, * P1, K5, rep from * to last 3 sts, K3.
2nd row: P3, *m1, K1, m1, P5 rep from * to last 3 sts, K3.
3rd row: K3, *P3, K5, rep from * to last 3 sts, K3.
4th row: P3, *K1,m1, K1, m1, K1, P5, rep from * to last 3 sts, P3.
5th row: K3, *, P5, K5, rep from * to last 3 sts, K3.
6th row: P3, *K2, m1, K1, m1, K2, P5, rep from * to last 3 sts, P3.
7th row: K3, * P7, K5, rep from * to last 3 sts, K3.
8th row: P3, *K7, P5, rep from * to last 3 sts, P3.
9th row: As 7th row.
10th row: P3, * Sl 1, K1, Psso, K3, K2tog, P5, rep from * to last 3 sts, P3.
11th row: K3, As 5th row.
12th row: P3, *Sl 1, K1, Psso, K1, K2tog, P5, rep from * to last 3 sts, P3.
13th row: As 3rd row.

14th row: P3 * Sl 1, K2tog, paso, P5. rep from * to last 3 sts. P3.

15th row: Knit.

16th row: Purl.

17th row: Knit.

Change to Mid Purple and work three rows as follows;

Knit 1 row, Purl 1 row, Knit 1 row.

Repeat the first 15 rows of the pattern again ending with the knit row.

Change to Mauve Aran and work one row Knit and one row Purl.

Next row: (right side facing) K1, K2tog, K2* K2tog, K4, rep from * to last 2 sts, K2tog. 25 sts.

Third Pattern Section

1st row: K2, * P1, K4, rep from * to last 2 sts K2.

2nd row: P2, *m1, K1, m1, P4, rep from * to last 2 sts, P2.

3rd row: K2, *P3, K4, rep from * to last 2 sts, K2.

4th row: P2 *K1, m1, K1, m1, K1, P4, rep from * to last 2sts, P2.

5th row: K2, *P5, K4, rep from * to last 2s ts, K2.

6th row: P2tog, *K2, m1, K1, m1, K2, P1, P2tog, P1, rep from * to last 2sts, P2tog.

7th row: K1, *P7, K3, rep from * to last st, K1.

8th row: P1, K7, P2tog, rep from * to last 7sts, K7, P1.

9th row: K1, *P7, K2, rep from * to last st, K1.

10th row: P1, * Sl 1, K1, paso, K3, K2tog, P2tog, rep from * to last st, P1.

11th row: K1, * P5, K1, rep from * to end.

12th row: P1, * Sl 1, K1, paso, K1, K2tog, P2tog, rep from * to last st, P1.

13th row: K1, *P3, K1, rep from * to end.

14th row: P1, *Sl 1, K2tog, paso, P1, rep from * to end.

15th row: *K1, P1, rep from * to end.

Break off yarn, thread through rem sts, pull up tightly and fasten off. Make another side to match.

Leaves (Make one of each color)

Using 2, 3.75mm (US 5, UK 9) double pointed knitting needles, and Aran yarn, cast on 3sts.

1st row: * Knit, do not turn work, slide sts to other end of needle and pull yarn firmly behind the work, rep from * until "I Cord" measures ¾ in (2cm), proceed as follows;

1st row: K1, yfwd, K1, yfwd, K1.

2nd and alt rows: Knit.

3rd row: K2, yfwd, K1, yfwd, K2.

5th row: K3, yfwd, K1, yfwd, K3.

7th row: K4, yfwd, K1, yfwd, K4.

9th row: K5, yfwd, K1, yfwd, K5.

11th row: K6, yfwd, K1, yfwd, K6.

13th row: K7, yfwd, K1, yfwd, K7. 17 sts

15th row: Sl 1, K1, paso, K15, K2tog.

17th row: Sl 1, K1, paso, K13, K2tog.

19th row: Sl 1, K1, paso, K11, K2tog.

21st row: Sl 1, K1, paso, K9, K2tog.

23rd row: Sl 1, K1, paso, K7, K2tog.

25th row: Sl 1, K1, paso, K5, K2tog.

27th row: Sl 1, K1, paso, K3, K2tog.

29th row: Sl 1, K1, paso, K1, K2tog.

31st row: Sl 1, K2tog, paso, fasten off.

To Make Up

Place the tea cosy pieces together, right sides facing. Stitch top section together and lower edges for approx. ½ in (1.5cm) turn the right way out and darn in all loose ends.

Sew the three leaves, evenly spaced to the top of the cosy.

My Little Pea Pod

Eight pea pods top this little tea cosy and a trail of peas drifts down one side. These gorgeous felt pea, measuring ½ in (1cm) in diameter are available from Etsy and are just divine. You can buy them in a range of plain greens or with dots of different color for a few extra jazzy peas.

SKILL LEVEL
Intermediate knitting skills

MEASUREMENTS
To fit a 2–3 cup tea pot

MATERIALS
- 1 x 2 oz (50 g) ball 8 ply Pure Wool Bright Green (DK)
- 1 x 2 oz (50 g) ball 8 ply Pure Wool Pea Green (DK)
- 1 x 2 oz (50 g) ball 8 ply Pure Wool Dark Green (DK)

- 1 pair of 5mm (US 8, UK 6) knitting needles
- 1 pair of 3mm (UK 11) knitting needles
- Wool needle for sewing up
- Polyester sewing cotton
- Sewing needle
- 50, ½ in (1cm) diameter felt green balls (available from www.etsy.com)

TENSION
16 sts and 23 rows to 4 in (10cm) of stocking st using 5mm (US 8, UK 6) knitting needles and yarn doubled.

*Note – Using 2 slightly different shades of green gives your tea cosy a lovely water color look and is more 3 dimensional in effect. The 2 shades do not have to be very different from each other.

Tea Cosy (Make 2 pieces)
Using 5mm (US 8, UK 6) knitting needles and 2 shades of green 8 ply, cast on 30 sts.
Work 4 rows of garter st, (every row knit).
Next: work 17 rows of st st, beg with a knit row.
Work 3 rows of garter st.
Next: Work 6 rows of st st.
Shape top
Next row: *K2, K2tog, rep from * to last 2 sts, K2. 23 sts
Work 5 rows st st, beg with a purl row.
Next row: *K2, K2tog, rep from * to last 3sts, K1, K2tog. 17 sts
Next row: Purl.
Next row: K2tog to last st, K1. 9 sts
Break of yarn, thread through rem sts, pull up tightly and fasten off.
Work other side to match.

To Make Up
With right sides together sew the top of the cosy together leaving an opening for the spout and the handle. Sew the lower edges together for approx.

1¼ in (3cm). Darn in all loose ends and turn the right way out. It is much easier to sew the pea pods on the top of the cosy if it is sitting on the tea pot.

Pea Pods (Make 9)

Using 3mm (UK 11) knitting needles and dark green 8 ply, cast on 1 sts.

Next row: K1, P1, K1 all into same st. 3 sts

Next row: P3.

Next row: Inc in 1st st, K1, inc in last st. 5 sts

Next row and alt rows: K1, P to last st, K1.

Next row: Inc in 1st st, K1, inc in last st. 7 sts

Work a further 21 rows without further inc. ending with a purl row.

Dec row Sl 1, K1, paso, K3, K2tog.

Next row and alt rows: K1, P to last st, K1.

Next row: Sl 1, K1, paso, K1, K2tog.

Sl 1, K1, paso, K3, K2tog.

Next row: Sl 1, K2tog, paso. Fasten off.

To Make Up

Stitch closed the top edge of each pea pod forming a slightly boat shaped receptacle for holding your peas. Each pea pod will hold four felt peas. Using polyester cotton and a sewing needle sew four peas into each pea pod. Position the eight pea pods with their tips at the center of the top of the cosy and radiating out evenly. Their other ends should just reach the garter stitch border. Stitch in position at either end to secure. Sew the final pea pod into a nice round shape, ensuring none of the peas pop out and sew over the top of all the pea tips to neaten the top.

Take a chalk pencil and draw a wavy line on one side of the lower half of the cosy from the garter stitch border towards the bottom edge. Stitch the remaining felt balls along this wavy line so that they are touching each other.

Mistake Rib Double 8Ply Tea Cosy

This chunky knit tea cosy is knitted in double 8 ply and provides great insulation for your tea pot. It is the basis for a few projects in this book as it provides a nice firm base for embellishment. Being a double knit you can mix your strands of yarn to produce a lovely variegated shade as in "Daffodil". Be careful not to split the stitches when you are knitting.

SKILL LEVEL
Basic knitting skills

MEASUREMENTS
To fit a 6–8 cup tea pot

MATERIALS
- 3 x 2 oz (50 g) ball of 8 ply Pure Wool in desired shade.
- Note – Yarn is used double throughout so you will need to wind off half of the third ball to make a small fourth ball or alternatively you can purchase a fourth ball. I used Cleckheaton Country. Equivalent (DK)
- I pair of 4mm (US 6, UK 8) knitting needles
- Wool needle for sewing up

TENSION
19 sts to 4in (10cm) worked over pattern on 4mm (US 6, UK 8) Knitting Needles

Tea Cosy (Make 2 Pieces the same)
Using 4mm (US 6, UK 8) knitting needles and 8 ply (DK) yarn held double, cast on 49 sts.
1st row: *K2, P2, rep from * to last st, K1.
Rep this row until work measures 5½ in (14cm).

Shape Top
Next row: K2, *P3tog, K1, rep from * to last 2 sts, K2.
Next row: K2, P2, *K1, P1, Rep from *, to last 2 sts, K2.
Next row: K1, *Sl1, K1, paso, rep from, * to last st, K1.
Next row: K1, Purl to last st K1.
Next row: K2tog to last st, K1.
Cast off.

To Make Up.
With right sides together join cast off stitches and 1 in (2.5cm) either side of this section using a back stitch or other neat seam. Join the lower edges for ¾ in (2cm) on either side. Darn in all ends. Turn the right side out. Your tea cosy is now ready for embellishment.

Pastel Pagoda

This tea cosy reminds me of the Pagoda in Kew Gardens, London. It is knitted in two pieces then the sides are joined together for the top shaping. The knitted pleats give the cosy a very structured feel which is softened by the use of pastel colors and fluffy mohair yarn. As an alternative you could use bright colors and a standard 12 ply yarn for the contrast ridges.

SKILL LEVEL
Intermediate knitting skills

MEASUREMENTS
To fit a 6–8 cup tea pot

MATERIALS
- 1 x 2 oz (50 g) ball of variegated 8 ply Pure wool (DK) I used Purple shades
- 3 balls of Cleckheaton 12 ply Wool Mohair. Colors used were Lilac, Geranium and Pink
- 1 pair of 4mm (US 6, UK 8) knitting needles
- 1 pair of 3.25mm (US 3, UK 10) knitting needles (for pleats)
- 2, 3.25mm (US 3, UK 10) double pointed knitting needles
- Wool Needle for sewing up

STRIPE PATTERN
Color sequence is:
Geranium
Pink
Lilac
*Note – Work tucks in color sequence as above and use variegated 8 ply for rows in-between tucks.

TENSION
22.5 sts and 29 rows measured over stocking stitch using 4mm (US 6, UK 8) knitting needles and 8 ply yarn

Tea Cosy
Using 4mm (US 6, UK 8) knitting needles and variegated 8 ply (DK) yarn, cast on 45 st.
Work 8 rows st st, beg with a knit row.
Next row: K1,*yfwd, K2tog, rep from * to end.
Work a further 9 rows st st beg with a purl row.
Next row: Purl.
Work 7 rows st st beg with a purl row.
1st Tuck – Geranium: Work 9 rows st st in this shade and then work the tuck row as follows.
Next row: Place RH needle in first st on LH needle as if to purl, then put a spare needle through the first st of the loops of the first row of contrast color on the wrong side. Purl it together with this st. Repeat right along the row. First tuck made.
Change back to variegated 8 ply and work another 8 rows st st.
Following the preceding sequence make two further tucks. One in Pink and the next in Lilac.

When the lilac tuck has been made. Work one row knit in variegated 8 ply.

Next row: * P1, P2tog, rep from * to end, leave these sts on a spare needle.

Work the other side to match.

Joining the 2 pieces

Knit across the first set of stitches to last st. Knit together with first st on spare needle. Knit to end.

Work 3 rows st st in variegated 8 ply beginning with a purl row.

Make a tuck – This will be in Geranium

Next row: Knit.

Next row: * P2tog, P1 rep from * to end. 40 sts

Work a further 2 rows st st.

Work a tuck – Pink

Next row: Knit.

Next row: *P2, P2tog, rep from * to last st, P1. 30 sts

Work 2 rows st st.

Work a tuck – Lilac

Next row: Knit.

Next row: *P2, P2tog, rep from * to end. 22 sts

Work 2 rows st st.

Work a tuck – Geranium

Next row: *P2tog, P2, rep from * to last 2sts, P2tog. 14 sts

Work 2 rows st st.

Work tuck – Lilac

Next row: Knit.

Next row: *P1, P2tog, rep from * to last st, P1.

Work Tuck

Next row: Knit.

Next row: P2tog to last st P1.

Next row: K2tog 3 times.

P3tog fasten off.

With right sides together stitch top seam being careful to match pleats. Join. Fold up lower edge and slip stitch into place. Join lower edges for 1¼ in (3cm).

Using 2, 3.25mm (US 3, UK 10) double pointed knitting needles and Mohair make an "I Cord" 7½ in (20cm) long.

Stitch the "I Cords" to the very top of the cosy and knot them at the lower end. Darn in any loose ends.

Pineapple Tea Cosy

This old fashioned tea cosy will take you right back to the 50s but if you look closely you will see that it has been given a little face lift with beautiful beading to the center of each blackberry stitch. This gives the pattern definition and makes it that little bit more special. If you can't be bothered just leave it off but I think it is worth the extra effort. Knitted in 8 ply (DK) the cosy is quick to knit and is not difficult.

SKILL LEVEL
Intermediate knitting skills

MEASUREMENTS
To fit a 6–8 cup tea pot

MATERIALS
- 1 x 2 oz (50 g) ball of Yellow 8 ply (DK) I used Cleckheaton Country (Main Color)
- ½ ball each 2 shades of green 8 ply (DK) for Leaves, Cleackheaton Country or something similar. You will not need the full amount. (Contrast Color)
- 1 pair of 4mm (US 6, UK 8) knitting needles
- Wool needle for sewing up
- Sewing cotton
- 1 packet of Mara George Yellow Glass Beads
- Beading needle

TENSION
28 sts to 4 in (10cm) worked over pattern using 4mm (US 6, UK 8) knitting needles

Tea Cosy (Make 2 pieces the same)
Using 4mm (US 6, UK 8) knitting needles and main color (yellow), cast on 46 sts. Work 6 rows st st.
Next row: * K1, yfwd, K2tog, rep from * to last st K1.
Work a further 6 rows st st, beg with a purl row.

Begin pattern
1st row wrong side: Knit.
2nd and 4th rows: Purl.
3rd row: P1, *, (K1, P1, K1) all into next st, P3tog, rep from * to last st, P1.
5th row: P1, * P3tog, (K1, P1, K1) all in to next st, rep from * to last st, P1.
Rows 2–5 for Patt.
Cont in Patt until work measures 5½ in (14cm) from picot row ending with a 5th row.
Shape Top of Tea Cosy
Next row: P1, *P3tog, rep from *to last st, P1. 24 sts
Next row: *P2tog, rep from * to end. 12 sts.
Cast off rem sts.

Inner and Outer Leaves

Inner Leaves
Using first contrast yarn (Green) and 4mm (US 6, UK 8) knitting needles, cast on 45 sts,
*1st row: (K1, P10 4 times, K1 turn.

Cont on these 9 sts.

2nd row: K2, (P1, K1) 3 times, K1.

Rep 1st and 2nd row 7 times.

17th row: (K1, P3tog) twice, K1.

18th row: K2, P1, K2.

19th row: K1, P3tog, K1.

20th row: K3.

21st row: P3tog, Fasten off *.

(Join yarn to rem sts and rep from * to * 4 times)

Outer Leaves

Using second contrast 8 ply (DK) Green 8 ply and 4mm (US 6, UK 8) knitting needles, cast on 45 sts.

Work as for inner leaves, however only rep 1st and 2nd rows 5 times instead of 7.

To Make Up

With right sides together join top seam and bottom seams for ¾in (2cm), leaving an opening for handle and spout. Join the ends of the cast on edges of the leaves together to form a ring. Sew the two sets of leaves together then gather up firmly. Stitch to the top of your cosy. It may be necessary to gather the top of the cosy a little to make the leaves sit up well. Darn in all loose ends.

SEWING ON THE BEADS

Using polyester sewing cotton and a beading needle, stitch a glass bead to the center of each circular pineapple stitch motif. Be sure to go through the center of the bead a few times to make sure it is very firmly attached. You do not need to end off after each bead as they are fairly close together but be carful not to pull the cotton too tightly, you don't want the cotton breaking as you put the cosy over your teapot and a shower of beads ensuing. Repeat for the other side of the cosy.

Rainbow Connection Tea Cosy

This striped tea cosy is a great one for inexperienced knitters as there is no shaping involved. It is fully lined so there is no danger of your teapot catching cold and the beautiful colors of Sirdar Snuggly Baby Bamboo really bring it to life. This cotton yarn is equivalent to 8ply or DK so you could easily substitute a wool or wool blend. I do not knit with acrylic as I find it hard on the hands and it is not very warm but it is certainly a more economical option. If you have not knitted with cotton before I would recommend knitting a tension square as it can feel a little different to wool.

MATERIALS
- 7 x 2 oz (50 g) balls of Sirdar Snuggly Baby Bamboo. (This is an 8 ply (DK) Cotton) Substitute with 8 ply wool if preferred.
- 1 pair of 4mm (US 6, UK 8) knitting needles
- Wool needle for sewing up.
- 1 m of 1.5cm wide ribbon of choice.
- Colors used were – Navy, Aqua, Bright Green, Yellow, Pink, Orange, and Red

COLOR SEQUENCE
The striped sequence is worked as follows:
Navy, Aqua, Bright Green, Yellow, Pink, Orange, and Red

TENSION
22 sts and 28 rows to 4 in (10cm) of stocking sts worked on 4mm (US 6, UK 8) knitting needles. Tension is important, check tension carefully before you begin your project.

Tea Cosy (Make 2 pieces the same)
Using 4mm (US 6, UK 8) knitting needles and Navy Cotton cast on 52 sts.

1st row: *K4 navy, K4 aqua, rep from * to end of row.

2nd row: * K4 navy, K4 aqua, rep from * to end of row.

Rep the 2 rows twice more.

Begin patt.

1st row: Knit – navy.

2nd row: Purl – navy.

3rd row: Knit – navy.

4th row: Knit – navy.

5th row: Knit – navy.

6th row: Purl – navy.

These 6 rows form patt. Keeping patt correct, work one complete color sequence and then one further navy stripe.

Work the 1st 4 rows of the next aqua stripe and then work the next row as follows:

Next row: * K1, yrn twice, K2tog, K2, repf from *to last st, K1.

Next row: Purl.

Work a further 3 more complete stripes.
Cast off.

Make another side to match.

Lining (Make two pieces the same)

There will be sufficient yarn to choose your lining color which is worked in 2 row stripes. The lining of this cosy is worked in Red and Orange.

Using 4mm (US 6, UK 8) knitting needles and Red 8 ply Cotton, cast on 52 sts.

Work 2 rows garter st.

Work 46 rows st st in stripes of 2 rows orange 8 ply cotton, 2 rows red 8 ply cotton.

Work 2 row garter st red 8 ply cotton. 50 rows in total.

Cast off.

Make another piece to match.

To Make Up

Place a lining piece wrong side facing on top of an outer piece. The top of a lining piece should end just below the row of holes for the ribbon. Pin in place all round. It can be helpful to use a finer yarn to stitch the lining into place. Once the linings have been stitched into place put the right sides of the tea cosy together and stitch the lower edges together for approx. 1 in (2.5cm). Stitch from ribbon holes to the top edge together on each side and then turn the right way out. Thread the ribbon through the holes starting at the center on one side. Pull up the gathers and tie into a bow. Finally, darn in any remaining ends.

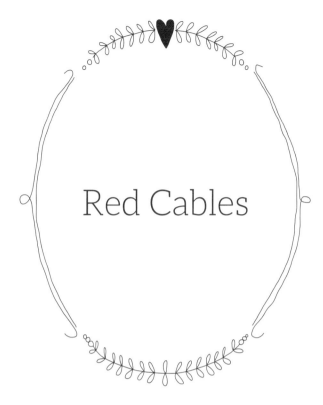

Red Cables

This simple looking tea cosy is a newt fit for your 6-8 cup tea pot. The cables converge beautifully to fit the top of the pot and it only takes 2 50 gram balls of 8 ply (DK) yarn to complete and yet looks very stylish. Make sure you keep all your cables crossing in the same direction for perfect symmetry and as always don't be bound by the color in the photo, Use your favorite color or if knitting as a gift, consider your friends favorite hues.

SKILL LEVEL
Intermediate knitting skills

MEASUREMENTS
To fit a 6–8 cup tea pot

MATERIALS
• 2, 2 oz (50 g) balls of 8 ply (DK Pure Wool, Red (I used Cleckheaton Country)

• 1 pair of 4.5mm (US 7, UK 7) knitting needles
• 1 Cable Needle
• Wool needle for sewing up

SPECIAL ABBREVIATION
Cable 6bck – Slip next 3 sts on to cable needle and hold at back of work, K3 the K3 from cable needle.

TENSION
20 sts to 4 in (10cm) over cable pattern on 4.5mm (US 7, UK 7) knitting needles

Tea Cosy (Make 2 pieces the same)
Using 4.5mm (US 7, UK 7) knitting needles and Red 8 ply (DK), cast on 50 sts.
Work 6 rows garter st. (Every row Knit)
Next row: Increase 4 sts evenly across row. 54 sts.
Begin pattern
1st row: *P4, K6, rep from * to last 4 sts, P4.
2nd row: *K4, P6, rep from * to last 4 sts, K4
3rd row: *P4, K6, rep from * to last 4 sts, P4.
4th row: *K4, P6, rep from * to last 4 sts, K4.
5th row: * P4, Cable 6bck, rep from * to last 4sts, P4.
6th row: *K4, P6, rep from * to last 4 sts, K4.
7th row: *P4, K6, rep from * to last 4 sts, P4.
8th row: *K4, P6, rep from * to last 4 sts, K4.
These 8 rows form patt.
Work in Cable pattern until the 5th cable has been completed ending with a 5th row.
Rep row 2.
Shape Top
1st row: (P2tog) twice, K6 rep from * to last 4 sts (P2tog) twice.
2nd row: K2, P6, rep from * to last 2 sts K2.
3rd row: *P2tog, K6, rep from * to last 2 sts, P2tog.
4th row: *K1, P6, rep from * to last st K1.
5th row: *P1, Cable, slip 3 sts on to a cable needle and hold at back of work, K2tog, K1, K2tog, K1 from Cable needle, rep from * to last st, P1.

6th row: *K1, P4, rep from * to last st, K1.

7th row: P1, (K2tog) twice, P1, rep from * to last st, P1.

8th row: * K1, P2, rep from * to last st, K1.

9th row: P1, * Sl 1, K1, psso, P1, rep from * to last st, P1.

10th row: P2tog 5 times.

Cast off.

With right sides together stitch top of tea cosy leaving an opening for the handle and spout. It can be useful to measure the pieces on your teapot prior to sewing to ensure a good fit. Sew the lower edges for approx. 1¼ in (3cm). Darn in all loose ends. Turn the right way out.

Remembrance Day

This striking black tea cosy is adorned with beautiful knitted poppies making a great contrast on top of the cosy. It would look wonderful with a simple white tea service. If you wanted to go all out, you could cover the whole cosy in knitted poppies but bear in mind that you would need extra yarn.

SKILL LEVEL
Advanced knitting skills

MEASUREMENTS
To fit a 6–8 cup tea pot

MATERIALS
- 3 x 2 oz (50 g) balls of 8 ply Pure Wool Black (DK)
- 1 x 2 oz (50 g) ball of 8 ply Red Pure Wool (DK)
- ½ a 2 oz (50 g) ball of mid green 8 ply Pure Wool (DK) for Poppy Center
- 1 pair of 4mm (US 6, UK 8) knitting needles
- Wool needle for sewing up
- 2, 3.25mm (US 3, UK 10) double pointed knitting needles

TENSION
19 sts to 4 in (10cm) measured over patterns using 4mm (US 6, UK 8) knitting needles

Tea Cosy (Make 2 pieces the same)
Using 4mm (US 6, UK 8) knitting needles and Black 8ply (DK) yarn held double, cast on 49 sts.
1st row: *K2, P2, rep from * to last st, K1.
Rep this row until work measures 5½ in (14cm).
Shape Top
Next row: K2, *P3tog, K1, rep from * to last 2 sts, K2.
Next row: K2, P2, *K1, P1, Rep from *, to last 2 sts, K2.
Next row: K1, *Sl1, K1, paso, rep from, * to last st, K1.
Next row: K1, Purl to last st K1.
Next row: K2tog to last st, K1.
Cast off.

To Make Up
Right sides together, join cast off stitches and 1 in (2.5cm) either side of this section using a back stitch. Join the lower edges for ¾ in (2cm) on either side. Darn in all ends. Turn the right side out. Your tea cosy is now ready for embellishment.

Poppies (Make 5 the same)
Using 2, 3.25mm (US 3, UK 10) double pointed knitting needles and Red 8 ply, cast on 7 sts.
1st row: Knit
2nd row: Inc in first st, Knit to last 2 sts, inc in 2nd last st, K1. 9 sts
3rd and 4th rows as 2nd row: 13 sts
Work 4 rows garter st.
9th row: (Sl 1, K1, paso) twice, knit to last 4 sts,

(K2tog) twice.

Knit 2 rows garter st.

12th row: as 9th row.

Knit 2 rows garter st,

15th row: K1, Sl 2, K1, paso, K1. 3 sts

16th row: Knit.

Cast off.

Center

Using 2, 3.25mm (US 3, UK 10) double pointed knitting needles and Green 8 ply cast on 16 sts. Cast off.

To Make Up

Sew petals together in pairs, then position one pair over the other in a cross formation and secure with some small stitches. Coil the center into a tight spiral and sew the base into the center of the flower. Using black 8 ply work a row of French Knots around the outer edge of the green center. Maintain the petals in a cup shape with a small stitch behind each pair of petals.

Stained Glass Windows Tea Cosy

The use of a simple slip stitch pattern and beautiful Noro Yarn produces this lovely variegated effect as you knit. One side is quite different from the other so if you like things to absolutely match this is not the tea cosy for you. Alternatively, choose two yarns with no variation. Although the pattern seems long you will quickly be able to memorize it.

Intermediate knitting skills

MEASUREMENTS
To fit a 6–8 cup tea pot

MATERIALS
- 1 x 2 oz (50 g) ball of Noro Yarn (Yarn A)
- 1 x 3½ oz (100 g) ball of Cleckheaton Californian (Yarn B)
- 1 pair of 4mm (US 6, UK 8) knitting needles
- 1 pair of 3.75mm (US 5, UK 9) knitting needles
- 2, 3.75 (US 5, UK 9) double pointed knitting needles
- Wool needle for sewing up.

TENSION
22 sts and 28 rows to 4 in (10cm) measured over slip st pattern on 4mm (US 6, UK 8) knitting needles

Tea Cosy (Make 2 pieces the same)
Using 4mm (US 6, UK 8) knitting needles and Noro yarn cast on 50 sts.
Work 6 rows garter st, (every row knit)
Commence Pattern
1st row: (right side) Knit, using Yarn A.
2nd row: Knit using Yarn A.
3rd row: Yarn B, K1, *K3, slip 2 purl wise (yarn at back), K3* repeat from * to * to last st K1.
4th row: Yarn B, K1, *P3. slip 2 purl wise, (yarn in front) P3* repeat from *to * to last st K1.
5th row: Yarn B, K1, *K3, slip 2 purl wise (yarn at back), K3* repeat from * to * to last st K1.
6th row: Yarn B, K1, *P3. slip 2 purl wise, (yarn in front) P3* repeat from *to * to last st K1.
7th row: Yarn B, K1, *K3, slip 2 purl wise (yarn at back), K3* repeat from * to * to last st K1.
8th row: Yarn B, K1, *P3. slip 2 purl wise, (yarn in front) P3* repeat from *to * to last st K1.
9th row: Knit, using Yarn A.
10th row: Knit, using Yarn A.
11th row: Using B, K1, *, slip 1 purlwise, (yarn at back), K6, slip 1 purlwise, (yarn at back) * repeat from *to *, K1.
12th row: Using B, K1, *slip 1 purlwise, (yarn in front), P6, slip 1 purlwise, (yarn in front) * repeat from *to *, K1.
13th row: Using B, K1, *, slip 1 purlwise, (yarn at back), K6, slip 1 purl wise, (yarn at back) * repeat from *to *, K1.
14th row: Using B, K1, *slip 1 purlwise, (yarn in

front), P6, slip 1 purlwise, (yarn in front) * repeat from *to *, K1.

15th row: Using B, K1, *, slip 1 purlwise,(yarn at back), K6, slip 1 purlwise, (yarn at back) * repeat from *to *, K1.

16th row: Using B, K1, *slip 1 purlwise, (yarn in front), P6, slip 1 purlwise, (yarn in front) * repeat from *to *, K1.

17th row: Knit using A.

18th row: Knit using A.

Repeat rows 3 to 18 inclusive.

Continue in pattern until work measures 5½ in (14cm) from cast on edge which will be approx. 3½ pattern repeats.

Break off Cleakheaton Californian (Yarn A) and continue in Noro (yarn B) only.

Shape Top

Next row: *K2, K2tog, rep from * to last 2 sts K2. 38 sts

Next row: Purl.

Next row: * K1, K2tog, rep from * to end K2. 26 sts

Next row: Purl.

Next row: K1, * Sl 1, K1, paso, rep from * to last st K1. 14 sts

Next row: Purl.

Next row: K2tog all across. 7 sts

Cast off.

Make another side to match.

Spout and Handle Ends

With right sides together join front side at top edge. Turn right way out. Using 3.75mm (US 5, UK 9) knitting needles and Noro Yarn and with right side facing pick up and knit 60 sts along spout edge. Work 6 rows garter st, Cast off. Repeat on the handle side. Fold in half and stitch together for the bottom ¾in (2cm). Darn in all loose ends.

"I Cord" Loops (make 7)

Using 3.75mm (US 5, UK 9) double pointed knitting needles and Cleckheaton Californian cast on 3 sts.

1st row: * Knit.

Do not turn, slide sts to the other end of the needle, pull yarn firmly behind the work and repeat the first row. Continue in this manner until your "I Cord" is 5½ in (14cm). To finish off. Sl 1 K2tog psso, fasten off.

Fold each "I Cord" loop in half and stitch to the top of the cosy creating a flower like shape.

Darn in any loose ends.

Sunflower Tea Cosy

This tea cosy is a contrast of color, the boldness of the black and the beautiful gold of the sunflower. The sunflower has been beaded in the center for added impact.

SKILL LEVEL
Intermediate knitting skills

MEASUREMENTS
To fit a 6–8 cup tea pot

MATERIALS
• 3 x 2 oz (50 g) balls of 8 ply Pure Wool Black (DK)
• 1 x 2 oz (50 g) ball of 8 ply Pure Wool Yellow (DK)
• 1 pair of 4mm (US 6, UK 8) knitting needles
• 1 x 3.5mm (US E/4, UK 9) crochet hook
• 3.6mm black glass beads
• Polyester sewing cotton
• Sewing needle

TENSION
19 sts to 4 in (10cm) measured over pattern using 4mm (US 6, UK 8) knitting needles

CROCHET ABBREVIATIONS
Ch – Chain
DC – Double Crochet
SS – Slip Stitch
TR – Treble Crochet
Slip Ring
HTR – Half Treble

Sunflower
Make center first
Using a 3.5mm (US E/4, UK 9) crochet hook and black 8 ply make 4ch, join into a ring with a sl st.
1st round: work 8dc into ring, join with a sl st.
2nd round: 1ch, 1dc into same dc, 2dc into each dc to end. 16dc.
3rd round: ch, 1dc into same dc, 2dc into each dc to end. 32dc.
Make another flower center the same.
Place the 2 flower centers together and work a row of dc through one of the chain loops on each of the outside dc loops of each round – 32dc. Darn in all ends.

Petals
Using a 3.5mm (US E/4, UK 9) crochet hook and yellow 8 ply, join with a sl st into any dc of flower center. 6ch, working sts in chain just made, dc in next ch from hook, 1htr, in next ch, 2tr in next ch, 1htr in next ch, 1dc in next ch, sl st, in next st of flower, repeat 16 times all round flower. 16 petals.

Second layer of petals
Worked behind first round.
Using 3.5mm (US E/4, UK 9) crochet hook and

yellow 8 ply work into the flower center just behind the first layer of petals.

Begin with a sl st and work each petal thus, ch10, dc into next ch from hook, htr into next 2 ch, 2tr into next 2ch, htr into next 2ch, dc into next 2ch, sl st behind next petal. repeat 16 times.

Using polyester cotton and 3.6mm glass beads stitch 2 rows of beads around the outer edge of the flower center.

Darn in any loose ends. Stitch the flower to the top of the tea cosy.

Tea Cosy (Make 2 Pieces the same)

Using 4mm (US 6, UK 8) knitting needles and Black 8 ply (DK) yarn held double, cast on 49 sts.

1st row: *K2, P2, rep from * to last st, K1.

Rep this row until work measures 5½ in (14cm).

Shape Top

Next row: K2, *P3tog, K1, rep from * to last 2sts, K2.

Next row: K2, P2, *K1, P1, Rep from *, to last 2sts, K2.

Next row: K1, *Sl1, K1, paso, rep from, * to last st, K1.

Next row: K1, Purl to last st K1.

Next row: K2tog to last st, K1.

Cast off.

To Make Up

With right sides together join cast off stitches and 1 in (2.5cm) either side of this section using a back stitch or other neat seam. Join the lower edges for ¾ in (2cm) on either side. Darn in all ends. Turn the right side out. Your tea cosy is now ready for embellishment.

The Big Blackberry

This tea cosy resembles a big blackberry. Ideal for an afternoon tea with scones and jam. It is knitted in doubled 8 ply and is an elegant structural shape.

SKILL LEVEL
Intermediate knitting skills

MEASUREMENTS
To fit a a 6–8 cup tea pot

MATERIALS
- 3 x 2 oz (50 g) balls dark purple 8 ply (DK) Pure Wool. I used Cleckheaton Country
- 1 x 2 oz (50 g) ball of leaf green 8 ply (DK) Pure Wool. I used Cleckheaton Country
- 1 pair of 4mm (US 6, UK 8) knitting needles
- 2, 4mm (US 6, UK 8) double pointed knitting needles
- Wool Needle for sewing up

TENSION
20 sts to 4 in (10cm) of patt measured on 4mm (US 6, UK 8) knitting needle with yarn used double.
*Note – it is quite hard to measure your tension with Blackberry Stitch and you are going to end up with a very firm knitted fabric. If you suffer from arthritis you may find going up to a 4.5mm (US 7, UK 7) knitting needle easier however the fabric will not be quite as firm or the pattern quite as defined.

Blackberry Stitch Pattern
1st row: Purl.
2nd row: K1, * ,(K1, P1, K1) all in to same st, P3tog, rep from * to last st, P1.
3rd and 4th row: Purl.
5th row: K1, *P3tog, (K1, P1, K1) all into same St, rep from * to last st, K1.
Repeat rows 2–5 inclusive.

Tea Cosy (Make 2 pieces the same)
Using 4mm (US 6, UK 8) knitting needles and Purple 8 ply (DK) yarn, held double, cast on 46 sts.
Work in Blackberry Stitch Pattern (See Above) for 5½ in (14cm), ending with a 3rd row.
Shape Top
Next row: K1, *K1, P3tog, rep from * to last last 2 sts, K2. 23 sts
Next row: Purl.
Next row: K1, *Sl 1, K1, paso, rep from * to end. 12 sts
Next row: Purl.
Next row: K2tog, 6 times. 6 sts.
Cast off. Make another side to match.

To Make up
Place the 2 sides of cosy together and stitch at the top leaving the cast off section open. Sew either side of this little hole for approx. 1½ in (4 cm). Stitch the lower edge closed for ½ in (1.5cm). Darn in any loose ends. Turn the right way out.

Leaf (Make 1)

Yarn is used double throughout.

Using 4mm (US 6, UK 8) knitting needles and Leaf Green 8 ply (DK) yarn, held double, cast on 5 sts.

1st row: Sl 1, yon, K2tog, yon, K2.

2nd row and alt rows: Sl 1, Knit to end.

3rd row: Sl 1, (yon, K2tog)twice, yon, K1

5th row: Sl 1, (yon, K2tog) twice, yon,K2

7th row: Sl 1, (yon, K2tog) three times, yon , K1

9th row: Sl 1, (yon,K2tog)three times yon, K2.

11th row: Sl 1, (yon, K2tog)four times, yon, K1.

13th row: Sl 1, (yon, K2tog),four times, yon, K2

15th row: Cast off 8 sts, yon, K2tog, yon, K1.

16th row: As row 2.

Rep rows 1–16 4 times, then cast off.

Stem

Using 4mm (US 6, UK 8) knitting needles and Leaf Green 8 ply (DK) yarn, held double, cast on 3 sts. Work an "I Cord" for 1½ in (4cm).

Next row: Sl 1, K2tog, paso, Fasten off.

To Make Up

Join the leaf section together at the inner edge for ¾ in (2cm). It will look like a crown. Next run a gathering thread around the inner edge. Gather up so that it will fit on top of the cosy. Before securing, catch in the stem. Sew the leaf to the top of the cosy, guiding the needle in and out through the hole created by the cast off stitches. Once it is securely in place, finish off and darn in any loose ends.

Tangerine Garter Stitch Tea Cosy

This is a simple but stylish tea cosy, if you are a beginner knitter this would be a good one to start on. Naturally you don't need to choose this color scheme but it does work well with natural wood buttons.

SKILL LEVEL
Basic knitting skills

MEASUREMENTS
To fit a 6–8 cup tea pot

MATERIALS
- 2 x 2 oz (50 g) balls of 8 ply (DK) Orange
- 1 x 2 oz (50 g) ball of 8 ply (DK) Dark Orange
- 2 x 1 ¼ in (3cm) Wooden buttons
- Sewing cotton and sewing needle
- Wool needle for sewing up
- 1 pair of 4mm (US 6, UK 8) knitting needles
- 1 pair of 3.75mm (US 5, UK 9) knitting needles

TENSION
16 sts and 38 rows to 4 in (10cm) measured over garter st on 4mm (US 6, UK 8) knitting needles

Tea Cosy (Make 2 pieces the same)
Using 4mm (US 6, UK 8) knitting needles and Orange 8 ply, cast on 54 sts.
Work in Garter st. (every row knit) for 6½ in (17cm).
Shape Top
Next row: * K3, K3tog, rep from * to last 3 sts, K3tog. 36 sts.
Next row: Knit.
Next row: K2to all across. 18 sts.
Next row: Knit.
Next row: * K2, K2tog, rep from * to end. 14 sts.
Cast off.
Make another piece to match.

Top Piece (Dark Orange)
Using 3.75mm (US 5, UK 9) knitting needles and Dark Orange 8 ply, (DK), cast on 12 sts. Work in garter st (every row knit) for 22 rows.
Cast off.

To Make Up
Place the two halves of the cosy together and stitch the cast off edges together. Turn the right way out. Wrap the dark orange piece around the stitched center and overlap at the top. Stitch through the center of this piece to hold in place.
Next, fold the outer top edge of each side 2 in (5cm) to the outside so that there is a seam in the center. Stitch through this seam. Place the 2 buttons on top of the dark orange piece and stitch in place using polyester sewing cotton or embroidery cotton. Sew the bottom 1 in (2.5cm) side seam closed on each side. Turn up the lower hem ½ in (1.5cm) and slip stitch in place. Darn in any loose ends.

The Big Grey Pom Pom Tea Cosy

Not everyone wants a bright and colorful tea cosy. Some homes have muted tones and there is always a place for this mock cable tea cosy with its lovely traditional pom-pom. I just love charcoal grey but feel free to choose any color you like.

SKILL LEVEL
Intermediate knitting skills

MEASUREMENTS
To fit a 6–8 cup tea pot

MATERIALS
- 2 x 2 oz (50 g) balls of 8 ply Charcoal Grey Pure Wool (DK)
- Small amount of Cream 8 ply (for Pom-Pom)
- Pom-Pom maker (2 in (5cm) of cardboard to cut 2 x 2 in (5cm) circles with the center cut out)
- 1 pair of 4mm (US 6, UK 8) knitting needles
- 1 pair of 3.25mm (US 3, UK 10) knitting needles
- Wool needle for sewing up

TENSION
22 sts and 30 rows to 4 in (10cm) measured over Pattern on 4mm (US 6, UK 8) knitting needles Measure tension carefully. If fewer sts try using one size smaller needles. If more sts try using one size larger needles.

SPECIAL ABBREVIATION
TW2L – slip next st onto a cable needle and hold at front of work purl next st from left hand needle then knit into back of stitch from cable needle.

TW2R – slip next stitch onto a cable needle and hold at back of work, knit into back of stitch from left hand needle then purl stitch from cable needle.

Tea Cosy (Make 2 pieces the same)
With 3.25mm (US 3, UK 10) knitting needles and Charcoal grey 8ply (DK), cast on 45 sts.
Work 4 rows garter st, (every row knit)
Next row: K4, *Inc in next st , K8, rep from * to last 5 sts, inc in next st, K4. 50 sts.
Change to 4mm (US 6, UK 8) knitting needles and begin patt.
1st row: K1, P2, *K4, P6, rep from * to last 7sts, K4, P2, K1.
2nd row: K3, *P4, K6, rep from * to last 7sts, P4, K3.
3rd row: K1, P2, * Tw2L, Tw2R, P6, rep from * to last 7sts, Tw2L, Tw2R, P2, K1.
4th row: As 2nd row.
5th row: K1, P2, *Tw2R, Tw2L, P6, rep from *, to last 7sts, Tw2r, Tw2L, P2, K1,
6th row: As 2nd row.
These 6 rows form patt.
Rep 6 patt rows 3 times more then rows 1 to 4 again.
Shape Top

1st row: K1, P2, *Tw2R, Tw2L, P2, P2tog, rep from * to last 7sts, Tw2R, Tw2L, P2, K1. 46 sts

2nd row: K3, *P4, K5, rep from * to last 7sts, P4, K3.

Keeping continuity of pattern work 2 rows.

Next row: K1, P2tog, *Tw2L, Tw2R, P1, P2tog, P2, rep from * to last 7sts, Tw2L, Tw2R, P2tog, K1. 40 sts

Next row: K2, *P4, K4, rep from * to last 6 sts P4, K2.

Keeping continuity of pattern work 2 rows.

Next row: K1, P1, *K4, P1, P2tog, P1, rep from * to last 6sts, K4, P1, K1. 36sts.

Next row: K2, *P4, K3, rep from * to last 6sts, P4, K2.

Keeping continuity of pattern work 2 rows.

Next row: K2tog, * Tw2R, Tw2L, P1, P2tog, rep from * to last 6sts, TW2R, Tw2L, K2tog. 30 sts

Next row: K1*P4, K2, rep from * to last 5 sts, P4, K1.

Next row: K5, *P2tog, K4, rep from * to last st, K1. 26 sts

Next row: K1, *P4, K1, rep from * to end.

Next row: K1, *K2togtbl, K2tog, P1, rep from * to last 5 sts, K2togtbl, K2tog, K1. 16 sts

Next row: K1, *K2tog, K1, rep from * to end. 11 sts

Next row: P1*P2tog, rep from * to end. 6 sts

Next row: K2tog 3 times.

Next row: P3tog, fasten off.

Make another piece to match.

To Make Up

With right sides together sew top leaving an opening for spout and handle. Sew lower edge closed for approx. 1 in (2.5cm). Darn in any loose ends. Turn the right way out.

Make a pom-pom for the top using a mixture of charcoal and cream yarn. Sew to the top of the cosy.

The Cupcake Tea Cosy

For all lovers of cupcakes this tea cosy is for you. Authentic in every way right down to the cherry on top. If you are not keen on beading for the hundreds and thousands you could achieve the same affect by stitching French Knots with embroidery cotton.

Intermediate knitting skills

MEASUREMENTS
To fit a 6–8 cup tea pot

MATERIALS
- 1 x 2 oz (50 g) ball 8 ply Pure Wool Bright Pink (DK)
- 1 x 2 oz (50 g) ball 8 ply Pure Wool Pale Pink (DK)
- 1 x 2 oz (50 g) ball 8 ply Pure Wool Biscuit (DK) *
  * **Note** this is for the picot edging less than whole ball will be used

- 1 x 2 oz (50 g) ball 8 ply Pure Wool Mustard (DK)
  * **Note** – this is for the picot edging less than whole ball will be used
- 1 x 2 oz (50 g) ball 8 ply Pure Wool Cream (DK)
- Small amount of 4 ply (fingering) red pure wool for Cherry
- Pink 3mm Glass beads for hundreds and thousands
- Polyester cotton and sewing needle
- Wool needle
- 1 pair of 4mm (US 6, UK 8) knitting needles
- 2, 2.75mm (US 2, UK 12) double pointed knitting needles

TENSION
18 sts to 4 in (10cm) worked over pattern using yarn doubled and 4mm (US 6, UK 8) knitting needles

Tea Cosy (Make 2 pieces the same)
Using 4mm (US 6, UK 8) knitting needles and 8 ply (DK) Pale Pink and Bright Pink yarn double, cast on 49 sts.

1st row: *K2, P2, rep from * to last st, K1.
Rep this row a further 23 times.
Break of Purple 8 ply and join in Biscuit/Mustard 8 ply double.
Work 4 rows st st.
Next row: Picot row – K1,*yfwd, K2tog, rep from * to end.
Work a further 4 rows st st beg with a purl row.
Next: Make a tuck by folding the picot row to the right side. Use a spare needle to lift the purl ridge from the first row and place it on the needle in front of the first st. Purl together with the first st. Repeat along the row. This creates the muffin top. Break off Biscuit/mustard and join in cream, held double.
Work a further 8 rows st st beginning with a knit row.
Shape Top
1st row: *K2tog, K6, rep from * to end of row.

2nd and alt rows: Purl.

3rd row: *K2tog, K5, rep from * to end of row.

5th row: *K2tog, K4, rep from * to end of row.

7th row: *K2tog, K3, rep from * to end of row.

9th row: *K2tog, K2, rep from * to end of row.

11th row: *K2tog, K1, rep from * to end of row.

13th row: K2tog all across. 6 sts

Cast off.

Make another piece to match.

Special instruction

Wrap 1: To minimize the hole made by turning in mid row, slip next st purl wise, take yarn to opposite side of work, slip st back on to left hand needle, ready to turn, and work next short row.

Cherry

Using 2.75mm (US 2, UK 12) double pointed knitting needles and Red 4 ply yarn, cast on 12 sts.

1st row: Knit.

2nd row: P10, wrap 1, turn.

3rd row: K8, wrap 1turn,

4th row: P6, wrap 1 turn,

5th row: K4, wrap 1 turn.

6th row: Purl all across.

Repeat these 6 rows a further 4 times. Cast off.

To Make Up – Cherry

With right sides together sew half the seam closed, running a gathering thread around one end. Turn the right way out. Stuff firmly and then Finish closing the seam. To shape the cherry, take a length of yarn and secure firmly at one end of the cherry, insert right through the cherry and then take it back through to the other end. Fasten off.

To Make Up

With right sides together sew the top together, leaving an opening for the handle and the spout. It can be a good idea to measure the pieces on your cosy before sewing to ensure a good fit. Sew the lower ends closed for approx. 1¼ in (3cm). Darn in all ends and turn the right way out. Using the photograph for guidance stitch the beads to the top of the cake. By using a matching thread and running the thread under the stitches you will not need to be ending off the thread after every bead. Just be careful not to pull your thread too tightly. Stitch the cherry to the center of the top of the cosy.

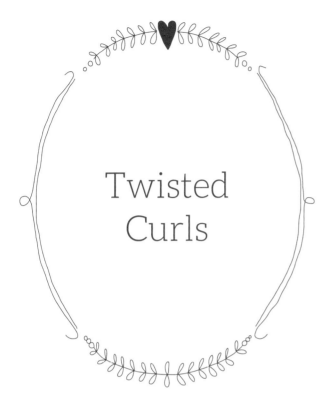

Twisted Curls

The glorious curly topknot on this tea cosy is made from King Cole Bamboozle. Don't be worried if you can't find this fancy yarn. There is an absolute proliferation of amazing colorful yarns on the market at the moment so just choose one to match your color scheme. You will not be using a whole lot of yarn so don't be too alarmed if some of them do seem a bit pricey you can always use the leftovers up for some other project.

SKILL LEVEL
Intermediate knitting skills

MEASUREMENTS
To fit a 6–8 cup tea pot

MATERIALS
- 1 x 3½ oz (100 g) ball of Patons Inca (Chunky, 14 ply)
- 1 x 1 oz (25 g) ball of Rowan Kid Mohair in matching shade
- 1 x 3½ oz (100 g) ball of King Cole Bamboozle (Fancy Yarn) (Chunky 14 ply plus)
- 1 pair of 4.5mm (US 7, UK 7) knitting needles
- 1 x 4mm (US G/6, UK 8) crochet hook
- Wool Needle for sewing up

TENSION
22 sts and 30 rows to 4 in (10cm) measured over Pattern on 4.5mm (US 7, UK 7) knitting needles Measure tension carefully. If fewer sts try using one size smaller needles. If more sts try using one size larger needles.

CROCHET ABBREVIATIONS
Ch – Chain
DC – Double Crochet
SS – Slip Stitch
TR – Treble Crochet
Slip Ring
HTR – Half Treble

Tea Cosy (Make 2 pieces the same)
Using 4.5mm (US 7, UK 7) knitting needles and Patons Inca and Rowan Kid Mohair together, cast on 42 sts.

1st row: *P2, K3, rep from *to last 2 sts, P2.
2nd row: *K2, P3, rep from * to last 2 sts, K2.
Rep these 2 rows until work measures 5½ in (14cm) from cast on edge ending with a 2nd row.
Shape Top
1st row: *P2, K3tog, rep from * to last 2sts, P2. 26 sts
2nd row: *K2, P1, rep from * to last 2sts, K2.
3rd row: * P2tog, K1, rep from * to last 2sts, P2tog. 17 sts
4th row: *K1, P1, rep from * to last st, K1.
5th row: P1, *Sl 1, K1, psso, rep from * to end. 9 sts.
6th row: P1, P2tog, 4 times. Cast off.

With right sides together sew top of cosy together leaving an opening for handle and spout.
Sew lower edges together for ¾ in (2cm). Darn in all loose ends and turn cosy the right

Twisted Curls (Make at least 8–9 Curls)
Using 4mm (US G/6, UK 8) crochet hook and King Cole Bamboozle make 40ch. Work 2dc into every ch. The strip will curl naturally.

Stitch one end of the curl to the center of the top of the cosy allowing them to spiral over the top and sides of the the tea cosy. Darn in any loose ends, being careful not to pull the curls straight.

Under The Christmas Tree Tea Cosy

This is a special cosy for Christmas day and will definitely fill you with festive cheer. Little Christmas trees are brightly desecrated with glass baubles and the traditional colors leave not doubt about the Christmas Message. Would make a great gift, complete with tea pot and a range of homemade goodies.

SKILL LEVEL
Intermediate knitting skills

MEASUREMENTS
To fit a 6–8 cup tea pot

MATERIALS
- 1 x 2 oz (50 g) ball of Pure Wool Red 8 ply (DK)
- 1 x 2 oz (50 g) ball of Pure Wool Cream 8 ply (DK)
- 1 x 2 oz (50 g) ball of Pure Wool Dark Green 8 ply (DK)
- Small amount White Eyelash yarn
- *** Note** Yarn is used Double throughout with the exception of eyelash yarn
- Small amount of polyester fiber filling
- 1 pair of 4mm (US 6, UK 8) knitting needles
- 1 pair of 3.25mm (US 3, UK 10) knitting needles
- 3.6mm Swarovski crystal red beads for Christmas Trees
- Red glass beads
- Wool needle for sewing up
- Sewing cotton
- Sewing needle

TENSION
19 sts to 4 in (10cm) measured over pattern using 4mm (US 6, UK 8) knitting needles

Tea Cosy (Make 2 pieces the same)
*Note: Yarn is used double throughout except for Eyelash yarn.

Using 4mm (US 6, UK 8) knitting needles and Red 8 ply yarn used double, cast on 42 sts. Work 6 rows garter st, (every row knit). Change to White Eyelash yarn (used single thread) and work 5 rows garter stitch. Break off Eyelash yarn and join back in Red yarn used double. Purl 1 row.

Next row: * P2, K3, rep from * to last 2 sts, P2.

Next row: *K2, P3, rep from * to last 2 sts, K2.

Rep last 2 rows until work measures 5½ in (14cm) from cast on edge, ending with a 2nd row. Break off red and join in Cream 8 ply used double.

Next row: K2, *K1, Sl 1, K1, psso, K3, rep from * to end. 34 sts.

Purl 1 row. Leave sts on a spare needle.

Work other side to match.

Once you have both sides work across as follows –

Knit across first set of stitches – K2, K2tog, cont knitting across second set of stitches in the same manner. 51 sts.

Next row: Purl.

Next row: *K1, K2tog, rep from * to end. 34 sts.
Next row: Purl.
Next row: K2tog all across. 17 sts.
Next row: Purl.
Next row: Sl 1, K1, paso, to last st, K1.
Next row: P2tog, 4 times, P1.
Cast off.

Christmas Trees (Make 6)

Using 3.25mm (US 3, UK 10) knitting needles and
dark green 8 ply (1 strand), cast on 13 sts.
Work 2 rows garter st. (every row knit).
Next row: Dec 1st at each end of the row.
Work 1 row garter st.
Next row: Dec 1st at each end of the row.
Work 3 rows garter st
Next row: Dec 1st at each end of the row.
Work 5 rows garter st.
Next row: Dec 1st at each end of the row.
Sl 1, K2tog, psso, fasten off.

To Decorate Christmas Trees

Using red polyester cotton and a sewing needle.
Sew a 3.6mm Swarovski red crystal to the top of
each tree and then sew a few red glass beads evenly
interspersed around each tree. Using the photo as
a guide stitch three trees to each side of the cosy.
It may be easier to do this before sewing the cosy
together. Ensure that all glass beads are sewn on
really firmly. You don't want them dropping into your
tea or small children pulling them off.

Special instruction

Wrap 1: To minimize the hole made by turning in
mid row, slip next st purl wise, take yarn to opposite
side of work, slip st back on to left hand needle,
ready to turn, and work next short row.

3 Red Snowballs

Knitted Pom-Pom

Using 3.25mm (US 3, UK 10) knitting needles and
red 8ply, (DK), cast on 12 sts
1st row: Knit.
2nd row: P10, wrap 1, turn.
3rd row: K8, wrap 1turn.
4th row: P6, wrap 1 turn.
5th row: K4, wrap 1 turn.
6th row: Purl all across.
Repeat these 6 rows a further 4 times. Cast off.

To Make Up – Pom-Pom

With right sides together sew half the seam closed,
running a gathering thread around one end. Turn
the right way out. Stuff firmly and then Finish
closing the seam. To shape the ball, take a length of
yarn and secure firmly at one end of the ball, insert
right needle through the ball and then take it back
through to the other end. Fasten off.

To Make Up

With right sides together stitch seam closed leaving
an opening large enough for the spout. Stitch lower
seams closed for approximately ¾ in (2cm). Darn in
all loose ends. Turn cosy the right way out.

Sew pom poms to the top of the tea cosy.

Wee Willie Winkie Tea Cosy

This tea cosy looks exactly like a night cap right down to the pom-pom. I have made a knitted pom-pom to facilitate easier washing of your cosy but you could substitute with the more traditional cosy if you prefer. I have made my cosy in blue and white which also matches my tea service but naturally you can choose any two colors you prefer.

SKILL LEVEL
Basic knitting skills

MEASUREMENTS
To Fit a 6–8 cup tea pot

MATERIALS
- 1 x 2 oz (50 g) ball of 8 ply (DK) Pure Wool in Blue, (I used Cleckheaton Country)
- 2 x 2 oz (50 g) balls of 8 ply (DK) Pure Wool in Cream, (I used Cleckheaton Country)

- 1 pair of 4mm (US 6, UK 8) knitting needles
- Small amount of Polyester fiber filling for Pom-Pom
- Wool needle for sewing up

TENSION
22 sts and 29 rows to 4 in (10cm) of Stocking st worked on 4mm (US 6, UK 8) knitting needles. Tension is important so please check your tension carefully. If fewer sts try using one size smaller needles. If more sts try using one size bigger needles.

STRIPE PATTERN
2 rows Cream, 2 rows Blue Stocking stitch. Note on Purl rows the first 4 sts and last 4 sts are knitted.

Tea Cosy
Note – sides are worked separately to the point where top shaping begins and then placed on one needle and top shaping is worked as one.

Using 4mm (US 6, UK 8) knitting needles and Cream 8 ply, (DK), cast on 54 sts.
Work 18 rows in K1, P1 Rib.
1st row: Cream – Knit.
2nd row: Knit first 4 sts Purl to last 4 sts Knit last 4 sts.
3rd row: Blue – Knit.
4th row: Knit first 4 sts, Purl to last 4 sts Knit last 4 sts.
Keeping stripe pattern correct work until stocking stitch section measures 3½ in (9cm).
Next row: Dec 4 sts evenly across row. 50 sts
Next row: Purl, leaving sts on a spare needle.
Work next side to match.
Shape Top
Keep Stripe pattern correct throughout
1st row: *K8, K2tog, rep from * to end. 90 sts
Work 5 rows st st beg with a Purl row.

7th row: *K7, K2tog, rep from * to end. 80 sts

Work 5 rows st st beg with a Purl row.

13th row: *K6, K2tog, rep from * to end. 70 sts

Work 5 rows st st beg with a Purl row.

19th row: *K5, K2tog, rep from * to end. 60 sts

Work 3 rows st st beg with a Purl row.

22nd row: * K4, K2tog, rep from * to end. 50 sts

Work 3 rows st st beg with a Purl row.

25th row: *K3, K2tog, rep from * to end. 40 sts

Work 5 rows st st beg with a Purl row.

30th row: *K2, K2tog, rep from * to end. 30 sts

Work 5 rows st st beg with a Purl row.

35tth row: *K1, K2tog, rep from * to end. 20 sts

Work 5 rows st st beg with a Purl row.

40th row: Work 2tog all across.

Work 5 rows st st beg with a Purl row.

45th row: Work 2tog all across.

Break off yarn, thread through rem sts, pull up
    tightly and fasten off.

Special instruction

Wrap 1: To minimize the hole made by turning in
mid row, slip next st purl wise, take yarn to opposite
side of work, slip st back on to left hand needle,
ready to turn, and work next short row.

Knitted Pom-Pom

Using 4mm (US 6, UK 8) knitting needles and
Cream 8ply, (DK), cast on 12 sts

1st row: Knit.

2nd row: P10, wrap 1, turn.

3rd row: K8, wrap 1turn.

4th row: P6, wrap 1 turn.

5th row: K4, wrap 1 turn.

6th row: Purl all across.

Repeat these 6 rows a further 4 times. Cast off.

To Make Up – Pom-Pom

With right sides together sew closed half the seam,
running a gathering thread around one end. Turn
the right way out. Stuff firmly and then Finish
closing the seam. To shape the ball take a length of
yarn and secure firmly at one end of the ball, insert
right through the ball and then take it back through
to the other end. Fasten off.

To Make Up

With right sides together stitch closed the shaped
seam of the hat section. Sew closed the ribbed
sections and fold in half to the outside. Catch closed
so that they don't keep falling open. Darn in all
loose ends. Sew the knitted pom-pom to the point
and fold the point to one side of the cosy, catching
invisibly in place with a few small stitches.

Wild Strawberries Tea Cosy

This tea cosy has a real 50s flavor about it with its sage green and dusky pink pleated exterior and embellishments of beaded strawberries and knitted leaves. The red and green "I Cords" have a Swarovski crystal beads attached to the end just for an added bit of sparkle. This is not a very difficult construction but the putting together does require a little patience to achieve a really good result.

Intermediate knitting skills

To fit a 6–8 cup tea pot

- 2 x 2 oz (50 g) ball of Sage Green 8 ply Pure Wool (Main Color)
- 2 x 2 oz (50 g) ball, Dusky Pink 8 ply Pure Wool (Contrast)
- 1 pair of 4mm (US 6, UK 8) knitting needles
- Wool needle for sewing up
- Small amount of Red 4 ply wool for strawberries and knitted red balls (less than 1 oz/25 g)
- Small amount of Mid Green 4 ply for Leaves
- 2 x 2.25mm (US 1, UK 13) double pointed knitting needles for Leaves and Strawberries
- Polyester fiber filling for strawberries
- I packet of Ribtex Red glass beads with a sufficiently large hole to thread on to 4 ply yarn, 54 needed for each strawberry www.ribtex.com.au
- 5 teardrop shaped Swarowski ½ in (1cm) Red Crystal Beads
- Sewing thread (Red)
- Sewing needle or Beading needle

The pleated fabric is created by the yarn not in use being pulled tightly across on the wrong side. It is important to do this on each row. Carry the yarn on the back of the work and right across to the ends of the work. It may seem a little slow to begin with but you will develop a rhythm. It may seem a little slow to begin with but you will develop a rhythm.
Note – You will make 2 pieces the same.

B1 – bring yarn to the front, slip the next st purlwise, slide bead along yarn so that it sits firmly against the knitted fabric, take yarn to back of work, ready to knit the next st.

Tea Cosy

Using 4mm (US 6, UK 8) knitting needles and Sage Green 8ply, cast on 98 sts. Work 8 rows garter st. (every row knit).
Begin patt.
1st row: K1MC, K6C, *K7MC, K7C, rep from * to last 7 sts. K6MC, K1C. As you knit pull the yarn

not in use very firmly behind, to draw up the pleats.

2nd row: K1C, K6MC, *K7C, K6MC, rep from * to last 7 sts, K6C, K1 MC. Keep yarn to the front in this row and continue to pull the yarn not in use tightly so that pleats remain firm.

These 2 rows form patt. Continue in patt until 48 rows have been worked.

Commence decreases – Right side facing.

1st row: K2togM, K3C, K2togC, *K2togM, K3M, K2togC, K3C, K2togC, rep from * to last 7 sts, K2togM, K3M, K2togC.

2nd row: K1C, K4M, * K5C, K5M, rep from * to last 5 sts, K4C, K1M.

3rd row: K2togM, K1C, K2togC, * K2togM, K1M, K2togM, K2togC, K1C, K2togC rep from * to last 5 sts, K2togM, K1M, K2togC.

4th row: K1C, K2M, * K3C, K3M, rep from * to last 3 sts, K2C, K1M.

5th row: K2togM, K1C, * K2togM, K1M, K2togC, K1C, rep from * to last 3 sts, K2togM, K1C.

6th row: K1C, K1M, * K2C, K2M, rep from *to last 2 sts, K1C, K1M.

7th row: (K2togM)twice, * K2togC, K2togM, rep from * to last 4 sts, (K2togC) twice.

Break off yarn, thread through rem sts, pull up tightly and fasten off.

Make another piece to match.

Darn in any loose ends. With right sides together, stitch from the center top down each side for approx. 2 in (5cm). Be sure to end off very firmly. Join sides together at the bottom edge, stitching up each side for approx. 1¼–1½ in (3–4cm). Turn right side out. Your cosy is now ready for embellishing.

First thread all the beads onto the 4 ply red yarn. Berry Body. Make one back and front.

Using 2.25mm (US 1, UK 13) double pointed needles and Red 4 ply cast on 3 sts.

1st row: ws – inc in 1st st, P1, inc in last st...5 sts.

2nd row: (k1, B1) twice, K1

3rd row: Inc in 1st st, P3, inc in last st. 7sts

4th, 6th & 8th rows: (K1, B1) to last st, K1.

5th row: Inc in 1st st, P5, inc in last st. 9sts.

7th row: Inc in 1st st, P7, inc in last st. 11sts.

9th,11th,13th, 15th, &17th rows: K1, P9, K1.

10th and 14th rows: K2, (B1, K1) to last st K1.

12th and 16th rows: (K1, B1) to last st, K1.

18th row: sl 1, K1 psso, (B1, K1) to last 3 sts, B1, K2tog. 9 sts

19th row: K1, P7, K1.

Cast off.

Using 2.25mm (US 1, UK 13) double pointed needles and Green 4 ply cast on 8 sls.

1st row: ws – Cast off 5 sts, k2. 3 sts

2nd row: K3, turn, cast on 5 sts. 8 sts.

Repeat 1st and 2nd rows 4 times. Cast off.

Sew strawberry together with right sides facing. Leave top open. Turn right way out. Stuff quite firmly with fiber filling. Roll the calyx and secure along the cast off edge. Sew to the top of the strawberry. Look at your strawberry carefully and ensure that it is a good shape.

Using 2.25mm (US 1, UK 13) needles and Red 4 ply, cast on 12 sts.

1st row: Knit.

2nd row: P10, wrap.

3rd row: K8, wrap.

4th row: P6, wrap.

5th row: K4, wrap.

6th row: Purl.

Rep these 6 rows a further 4 times. Cast off.
With right sides together sew side seam half way.
Turn the right way out and stuff firmly. Sew the
remainder of the seam and then run a gathering
thread around the cast on edge. Pull up firmly and
fasten off. Do the same with the other end. Making
sure you have sufficient filling and have made a nice
round firm ball. Make 2 more balls the same.

Leaves (Make 8)

Using 2, 2.25mm (US 1, UK 13) double pointed
knitting needles, and Green 4 ply, cast on 3 sts.

1st row: * Knit, do not turn work, slide sts to other
end of needle and pull yarn firmly behind the
work, rep from * until "I Cord" measure ¾ in
(2cm), proceed as follows:

1st row: K1, yfwd, K1, yfwd, K1.

2nd and alt rows: Knit

3rd row: K2, yfwd, K1, yfwd, K2.

5th row: K3, yfwd, K1, yfwd, K3.

7th row: K4, yfwd, K1, yfwd, K4

9th row: K5, yfwd, K1, yfwd, K5.

11th row: K6, yfwd, K1, yfwd, K6

13th row: K7, yfwd, K1, yfwd, K7. 17 sts

15th row: Sl 1, K1, paso, K15, K2tog

17th row: Sl 1, K1, paso, K13, K2tog

19th row: Sl 1, K1, paso, K11, K2tog

21st row: Sl 1, K1, paso, K9, K2tog

23rd row: Sl 1, K1, paso, K7, K2tog

25th row: Sl 1, K1, paso, K5, K2tog

27th row: Sl 1, K1, paso, K3, K2tog

29th row: Sl 1, K1, paso, K1, K2tog

31st row: Sl 1, K2tog, paso, fasten off.

Make another 7 leaves to match. If you which you
can make some of the leaves smaller by beginning
the decreases at row 5 or 6 instead of row 7.

"I Cords" (Make 5 – 3 Red, 2 Green)

Using 2, 2.25mm (US 1, UK 13) DPNs, and Green or

Red 4 ply, cast on 3 sts.

1st row: * Knit, do not turn work, slide sts to other
end of needle and pull yarn firmly behind the
work, rep from * until "I Cord" measures 4 ½ in
(12cm).

Next: Sl 1, K2tog, psso. Fasten off.

To Make Up

Darn in one end, leave the other for attaching to the
top of the tea cosy.

Take one red Swarovski crystals and attach to the
end of the "I Cord" with the beading needle and
sewing thread. It is easier to do this by passing the
needle through the crystal bead and then through
a red glass bead. You can then just pass the needle
and thread back through the crystal and fasten off
securely at the end of the "I Cord"

* Note – It is easier to attach all the
embellishments to the top of the cosy if it is actually
sitting on a tea pot.

Attach the "I Cords", alternating the red and green
to the very top of the tea cosy once you have joined
it together and darned in any loose ends.

Next place the 8 leaves around the top of the tea
cosy, fanning out in a circular fashion. Use one end
of the leaves to sew to the top of the tea cosy and
darn the other end in securely.

Finally place the three Strawberries (with the calyx's
pointing up) and the three knitted balls on top of the
leaves, alternating a strawberry with a knitted ball
so that they sit in a nice little cluster in the center
of the top of the cosy. Ensure everything is stitched
in place very securely. Take a final look at your cosy
to ensure your embellishments are symmetrical.
Make a cup of tea and admire your beautiful
handiwork.

Starfish

When I finally finished this tea cosy I could not decide if it looked more like a sea anemone or a starfish but I think the starfish won out. The cosy is composed of individual knitted 3D triangles which are filled with polyester fiber filling just before the final round. Then stitched together in rows with 4 across the top to create this amazing geometric tea cosy. It is a great little carry along project as you need to make a total of 28 triangles to complete the cosy. Naturally you don't need to use shades of blue you can choose anything you like and it is a great project for using up small amounts of ends of balls. One thing that is good to do though is to make the bases all the same shade as this gives a unifying structure to the work.

SKILL LEVEL
Advanced knitting skills (patience needed in finishing)

To fit a 6–8 cup tea pot
Each Triangle measures
2 in (5cm) at the base and 2 ½ in (6cm) high

MATERIALS
- 3 x 2 oz (50 g) balls of main color 8 ply for base of triangles (you won't quite need the whole 3 balls but you need more than 2) I used navy blue.
- Small amounts of 8–9 shades of 8 ply in toning colors for tops of triangles. I used blues and purple.
- Polyester fiber filling
- 1 set of 5, 3mm (UK 11) double pointed knitting needles
- Wool needle for sewing up

TENSION
*Note – 8 ply is being knitted on smaller than normal needles here to produce a firm knitted fabric. The exact tension is not crucial but you want the knitted fabric to be firm. My suggestion is to complete your first triangle, stuff it and measure it to see that it comes up to the correct dimensions.

Triangles (Make 28)
Using a set of 4, 3mm (UK 11) double pointed knitting needles, and main color 8 ply, (you will change to 5 later), cast on 8 sts, 3, 2, 3. Join in to a ring being careful not to twist the stitches.
Knit one round.
2nd round: Inc in every st, 16 sts. Now spread sts over 4 needles and knit with the 5th needle.
3rd round: Knit.
4th round: On each needle – Inc in the first and last st, knit the other sts.
5th round: Knit.
Repeat the 4th and 5th rounds until there are 12 sts on each needle, 48 sts.

Next round: Purl.

Work a further 2 rounds in st st. Base of triangle is now complete. Break off base color and join in 8 ply color you have chosen for main part of triangle.

1st round: Knit.

2nd round: On each needle Sl 1, K1, psso, knit to last 2 sts, K2tog.

3rd and 4th rounds: Knit.

Repeat rounds 2, 3 and 4 until 4 sts rem on each needle.

Stuff triangle very firmly.

Next round: Sl 1, K1, psso, K2tog, on each needle.

Next round: K2tog on each needle.

Break off yarn, thread through rem sts pull up tightly and fasten off. At this point it is also a good idea to darn in all the loose ends as then you won't need to do this when you are sewing your triangles together.

Make a further 27 triangles – It seems like a lot but they are remarkably quick to make. When stuffing each triangle, it is a good idea to have a ready made one handy so you can ensure that you are getting them all the same size. Likewise, when choosing yarn for the project, try to use wool with a similar feel. Some wool has a percentage of acrylic in and will stretch when you stuff it and not hold a nice triangular shape. I would try to use pure wool. Clechheaton Country or Heirloom 8 ply.

Making up

Each side of the tea cosy will have 4 rows of 3 triangles with an extra triangle at the top of 1 and 4. Lay your triangle out and arrange them to determine the color scheme you prefer. You may need to jot this down on a piece of paper like a little map.

To sew the triangles – stitch 2 bases together creating a pair. Now stitch the next base to the

pair created. You will have three triangles in a line. Repeat this creating a piece 4 triangles wide by 3 triangles high. For the two top triangles, their base is sewn to the base of the first row and the base of the second row. Repeat this at the other end. You will see that this slightly curves the sides in. Repeat the sewing up pattern for the other side. Then finish off by stitching down the remaining open seams of the top triangles.

To create the opening for the spout and the handle you will need to stitch up ¾ in (2cm) on the base of the 2 side triangles where they meet and stitch down ¾ in (2cm) on the 2 side triangles where they meet. Repeat on the other side.

Arrow is pointing to base of cosy. Stitch up approx. ⅔ in (2cm) on each side to create opening for spout and handle on each side. Repeat at the top of the cosy. The two top triangles will be stitched together at the base drawing sides in.

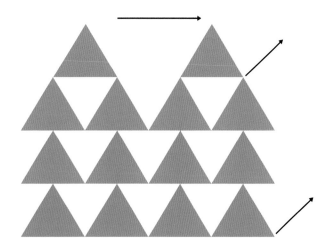

135

First published in 2016 by New Holland Publishers Pty Ltd
London • Sydney • Auckland

The Chandlery Unit 704 50 Westminster Bridge Road London SE1 7QY United Kingdom
1/66 Gibbes Street Chatswood NSW 2067 Australia
5/39 Woodside Ave Northcote, Auckland 0627 New Zealand

http://www.newhollandpublishers.com

ISBN 9781742578415

Managing Director: Fiona Schultz
Publisher: Diane Ward
Project Editor: Holly Wilsher
Designer: Lorena Susak
 Production Director: Olga Dementiev
Printer: Toppan Leefung Printing Limited

10 9 8 7 6 5 4 3 2 1

Keep up with New Holland Publishers on Facebook
www.facebook.com/NewHollandPublishers